M000295321

THE HISTORY OF THE
PANZERJÄGER

VOLUME 2: FROM STALINGRAD TO BERLIN 1943–45

OSPREY
PUBLISHING

PAI

Thomas Anderson

THE HISTORY OF THE
ZERJÄGER

VOLUME 2: FROM STALINGRAD TO BERLIN 1943–45

OSPREY PUBLISHING
Bloomsbury Publishing Plc
Kemp House, Chawley Park, Cumnor Hill, Oxford OX2 9PH, UK
1385 Broadway, 5th Floor, New York, NY 10018, USA
E-mail: info@ospreypublishing.com
www.ospreypublishing.com

OSPREY is a trademark of Osprey Publishing Ltd

First published in Great Britain in 2020

ISBN: HB 9781472836847; eBook 9781472836854; ePDF 9781472836823; XML 9781472836830

20 21 22 23 24   10 9 8 7 6 5 4 3 2 1

Conceived and edited by Jasper Spencer-Smith.
Design and artwork: Nigel Pell.
Index by Shaun Barrington.
Produced for Bloomsbury Plc by Editworks Limited, Bournemouth BH1 4RT, England
Printed and bound in India by Replika Press Private Ltd.

Front cover upper image: a 5cm PaK in service with 14.*Waffen-Grenadier-Division* (see page 276) (Getty); lower image: a Tiger in action on the Eastern Front.

Back cover, top to bottom: an anti-tank team with *Panzerfaust* (see page 209); a Marder II (see page 98); a 7.5cm PaK 40 (see page 92); an 8.8cm PaK 43/1 gun on a SdKfz 164 (see page 170).

Osprey Publishing supports the Woodland Trust, the UK's leading woodland conservation charity.

To find out more about our authors and books visit www.ospreypublishing.com. Here you will find extracts, author interviews, details of forthcoming events and the option to sign up for our newsletter.

CONTENTS

Introduction

In the 1920s, the concept of mechanized (mobile) warfare was born and the light tank became an essential item in the inventory of many armies around the world. Many deployed the tank as armoured cavalry – parades and manoeuvres looked impressive – but by the late 1930s the concept of a mass charge by armoured cavalry was outmoded. However, military commanders in Germany had thoroughly appraised the capabilities of the tank and began to assemble a well-organized, well-trained and effective armoured force. The result of their forward thinking and planning was seen in the *Blitzkrieg* (lightning war) on Poland in 1939, the advance through The Low Countries and the conquest of France in 1940.

After the first tanks were deployed on the battlefield in World War I, the military was faced with finding a method of halting these dangerous war machines. This resulted in military planners contracting armaments manufacturers to design and develop effective anti-tank guns and ammunition that could penetrate armour.

Many nations, including Poland, France, Great Britain and Russia placed reliance on artillery units equipped with light field guns. These weapons had a low trajectory and a relatively high muzzle velocity, which made it quite feasible for the type to be used against armoured targets.

After the end of World War I, German military planners decided that the light field gun was obsolete and ordered the production of more howitzers. Although the type had a low muzzle velocity (reducing ballistic performance) it was an essential support weapon for an advancing army, but was never effective as an anti-tank gun.

For this reason, the German armaments industry was ordered to design and develop anti-tank guns and also anti-tank weapons specifically for the infantry. In 1939, the *Wehrmacht* had in their inventory a considerable number of 3.7cm TaK (PaK), and also *Panzerbüchse* 39.

A *Panzerschreck* team waiting to ambush Soviet armour at Willkowischken (Vilkaviškis, Lithuania); the town was among the first to be overrun by advancing Russian forces in 1944.

By January 1941, the *Chef Heeresrüstung und Befehlshaber der Ersatzarmee* (Chef Hrüst und BdE – Chief of Army Ordnance and Commander of the Replacement Army) had registered a number of complaints with regard to the poor performance of divisional weapons:

Anti-tank weapons:

a) The 7.92mm *Panzerbüchse* [PzB] 39: Armour penetration is regarded to be seriously insufficient. A new type of anti-tank rifle has to be developed urgently.

b) 2.8cm s PzB 41: The mechanical design is still impractical. It is not intended to integrate this weapon into the *InfanteriePanzerjägerKompanie* [InfPzJgKp – infantry anti-tank company], since the 5cm *Panzerabwehrkanone* [PaK – anti-tank gun] has a superior performance. Also, the high-explosive (HE) ammunition lacks power.

c) The 3.7cm PaK is outdated as an anti-tank gun, but it is considered to be essential as an infantry support weapon.

d) The 5cm PaK is in the process of being issued to all InfPzJgKp at a rate of 12 guns per company.

e) The development of the Gerät 2472 must be continued, but the delivery date remains unconfirmed.

Two months later in March 1941, this expert opinion was corroborated by the *Oberkommando des Heeres* (ObdH – Commander-in-Chief of the Army):

A column of self-propelled PzJg 38(t) mounting the Russian-built M1936 (F-22) divisional gun, which was designated as the 7.62cm PaK 36(r) in German service. The gun (large numbers had been captured in the first months of *Unternehmen* (Operation) Barbarossa was re-chambered to fire the more effective German 7.5cm PaK 40 ammunition.

The German war machine became more reliant on captured equipment as the war progressed. A *Panzerjäger* team from an unknown unit has been equipped with a French-built 4.7cm PaK 181(f) towed by a Morris Commercial CS8 (Ersatz-Kfz 15), possibly one of the many abandoned by British forces at Dunkirk.

a) The *Schützenkompanie* [rifle companies] must be provided with an effective anti-tank weapon. This must have a calibre of 12–15mm, be operated by a two-man crew and be capable of penetrating 40mm armour at a range of 300m.

b) The present 3.7cm PaK must be improved without increasing the weight of the gun and its effective flat-trajectory fire.

c) The 5cm PaK 38 is too heavy and so weight must be considerably reduced. Also, if possible, the explosive power of both armour-piercing and high-explosive ammunition needs to be increased.

d) Development of the Gerät 2472 must be continued, but the weapon does require effective high-explosive ammunition.

[Note: The Gerät 2472 later became the 4.2cm PaK 41 and had a conical-type barrel (tapering from 42 to 27mm). Only a small number entered service due to a severe lack of tungsten carbide.]

Both reports were written before the invasion of the Soviet Union and indicate that senior military officials considered any fundamental changes to be unnecessary. Possibly they were aware of the production difficulties being experienced in the German armaments industry; a situation that continued until 1945.

When *Unternehmen* (Operation) Barbarossa was launched on 22 June 1941, the majority of *Panzerjäger* units were equipped with the 3.7cm PaK 36; some 14,500 were in service. Deliveries of the more powerful 5cm PaK 38 had begun in mid-1940, but only around 1,000 had been delivered by June 1941. Also available to anti-tank units were 500 Czech-built 4.7cm PaK.

The effectiveness of German anti-tank defences was drastically reduced when the Soviet T-34 medium and KV heavy tanks entered the battlefield; effective combat against these new types was no longer a certainty. The troops had to improvise and were forced to use light and heavy field artillery, including the formidable 8.8cm *Flugzeugabwehrkanone* (FlaK – anti-aircraft [AA] gun). But a courageous anti-tank mission by a close-combat team was often the last way of halting a heavily-armoured Soviet tank.

While design and development work continued on current weapons as planned, the *Waffenamt* (ordnance department) had already issued contracts for the development of heavier anti-tank guns, ignorant of the existence of the T-34 and KV. One contract was for the 8.8cm FlaK 36 to be developed as

The 7.5cm PaK 97/38 was the result of a search for an effective anti-tank weapon capable of defeating the latest well-armoured Russian tanks. The gun was an amalgamation of parts; the gun assembly was taken from a French-built 75mm *Canon de 75 modele* 1897 and mounted on the same split-trail carriage being produced for the 5cm PaK 38. The gun was fitted with a muzzle brake to improve performance.

an anti-tank weapon. Other technically more complex weapons, including a 7.5cm weapon taper-bore gun, were to be developed.

Despite the new threat posed by heavier and more mobile Soviet tanks the situation on the *Ostfront* (East Front) was stabilized, and the advance to Moscow continued apace.

Finally, the *Heereswaffenamt* (HWA – army ordnance department) had become aware – supported by a vast number of complaints from front-line commanders – of the true realities on the battlefront. As a result, the programme to develop a *schwere Panzerabwehrkanone* (s PaK – heavy anti-tank gun) was initiated.

Anti-tank Weapons – 1942

In early 1942, just six months after the sudden invasion of the Soviet Union, a number of newly developed weapons were deemed ready for production.

Conventional Weapons: German

7.5cm PaK 40

In February 1942, Rheinmetall-Borsig began delivering the 7.5cm PaK 40: the first truly 'modern' German anti-tank gun. The weapon was to become the

The 7.5cm PaK 40 was the first German high-velocity anti-tank gun capable of defeating the T-34 medium and the KV-1 heavy tank at long range. The marking stencilled on the gun shield indicates that it is in service with 168.InfDiv. The weapon is attached to a French-built Renault UE *Chenillette* (small tracked vehicle).

standard ordnance for anti-tank units, and was also mounted in the PzKpfw IV medium tank and the *Sturmgeschütz* (StuG – assault gun).

Conventional Weapons: Foreign

The lack of materials and capacity in the German armaments industry restricted any planned increase in the production of 7.5cm PaK 40. Furthermore, a number of guns were destined to be installed in tanks and assault guns. To compensate, the HWA ordered all captured equipment to be modified to use German ammunition.

7.62cm PaK 36

The Soviet 76mm M1936 (F-22) divisional gun is considered to be one of the best weapons used in World War II. During the initial phase of *Unternehmen* Barbarossa, German forces captured large numbers of the type in undamaged condition. Designated as the 7.62cm *Feldkanone* (FK – field cannon) 296(r), a significant number were used – firing Soviet ammunition – by German units. In June 1942, it was reported that 129 of the type were in service.

To optimize the FK 296(r) as an anti-tank weapon, it was modified by re-boring the breech chamber to fire superior German PaK 40 ammunition and fitted with a muzzle brake, and also a gun shield. The gun was designated 7.62cm PaK 36. Wartime documents note that the modifications were carried out by front-line workshop units; only the muzzle brake was delivered by the *Waffenamt*.

By 1 June 1942, some 229 guns had been modified and delivered. A significant number – possibly 698 – were diverted for usage on *Selbstfahrlafette* (Sfl – self-propelled [SP]) guns.

The Russian 76.2mm divisional gun M1936 (F-22) was one of the most versatile weapons in service during World War II. German military planners, impressed by its ballistic performance, immediately initiated modifications so that German ammunition could be fired. Designated 7.62cm PaK 36(r) it was issued in large numbers to front-line units.

A 7.5cm PaK 97/38 in service with an anti-tank unit attached to *Heeresgruppe Nord*. A well-prepared gun position could only be constructed when sufficient time and materials were available.

7.5cm PaK 97/38

In 1939, France had large numbers of the 75mm *Canon de 75 mle 1897*, quick-firing (QF) light field gun, despite it having entered service in 1898. By the time France capitulated in 1940, the *Wehrmacht* had captured large numbers of the type and issued them to units as the 7.5cm FK M 97(f). The critical situation with the supply and production of weapons, from 1941 to 1942, caused the *Waffenamt* to order the type to be modified for use as an anti-tank gun. This was made feasible because hollow-charge armour-piercing ammunition was beginning to be produced, which would compensate for the gun having a relatively low muzzle velocity. To improve mobility, the gun barrel and cradle were mounted on the split-trail-type carriage of the 5cm PaK 38. To improve performance the gun was fitted with a muzzle brake. By October 1942, the number of 7.5cm PaK 97/38(f) produced reached some 2,000.

Taper-bore Weapon

Adolf Hitler would often take an interest in and influence the development of military equipment. He appeared to be fascinated with modern technology;

in his eyes heavier and more sophisticated weapons would revitalize German industry and, ultimately, save the Reich. One such weapon was the taper-bore gun which, due to the shape of the barrel, fired projectiles at a high muzzle velocity. When compared to a similar anti-tank round, the (sub-calibre) type had a superior penetration capability.

To use this weapon effectively, tungsten carbide armour-piercing ammunition was required, but this was classified as *Mangelmaterial* (material in short supply). High-explosive ammunition was ineffective due to the small size of the shell.

Three types of taper-bore gun entered front-line service:

2.8cm s PzB 41

This anti-tank weapon was introduced primarily for *leichte Infanteriedivsionen* (le InfDiv – light infantry divisions) and *Gebirgsdivisionen* (GebDiv – mountain divisions). Field units of the *Luftwaffe* were also supplied with the weapon. A total of 150 were manufactured.

7.5cm PaK 41

Manufactured by Krupp, this anti-tank gun was the type of weapon desired by front-line troops. Armour 140mm thick could be penetrated at a range of 1,000m, so that now every type of Soviet tank could be defeated. Deliveries began on 1 June 1942, and production ended after 150 had been manufactured; more would have been built had it not been for the shortage of tungsten carbide.

Throughout World War II, engineers working in the German armaments industry sought innovative ideas when developing more powerful weapons. One development, the 7.5cm PaK 41, was designed using tape-bore technology. The high-performance gun entered service in summer 1942, but the constant shortage of tungsten-carbide ammunition affected its deployment.

The 7.5cm PaK 97/38 fired mainly German ammunition: the *Kopfgranate-Panzer* (KGrPz), an armour-piercing round which had been developed for the 7.5cm KwK L/24, and the *Panzer-Granate-Patrone* (PzGrPatr) 38 HL/B, a hollow-charge round. The standard high-explosive round was the 7.5cm Granate M15(f) captured French ammunition. The term *Patrone* indicates that it is a cartridge-type round.

The 7.5cm PaK 40 not only had a good ballistic performance, but its low profile made it easy to conceal on the battlefront. Note the double-layer gun shield which provided some protection for the crew against armour-piercing ammunition fired by enemy infantry and shrapnel.

4.2cm PaK 41

This taper-bore weapon was intended to supplement the 3.7cm PaK. It utilized the same carriage and gun shield, keeping it within required weight limits to ease transportation. Most were supplied to light infantry divisions and mountain divisions as initially planned. In February 1942, it was decided to issue the type to *Luftwaffe* field units. However, 1.GebDiv and 4.GebDiv and 97.le InfDiv and 100.le InfDiv were the only units to receive this weapon. The vast majority of tank destroyer units remained equipped with the 3.7cm PaK 36.

The 4.2cm PaK 41 programme also suffered from the ever-present shortage of tungsten carbide ammunition. By the end of the war some 151 guns had been produced.

Units: Organizational Issues

While waiting for the delivery of sufficient numbers of new weapons, front-line troops were again forced to improvise.

In December 1941, it was reported that the number of 3.7cm PaK operational (on all fronts) was some 12,288; six months earlier it had been 14,459. The total number of 5cm PaK 38 operational was 1,821; an increase of some 800 since June 1941.

A good example for this period is the following order of *Heeresgruppe Mitte* (Army Group Centre) dated 10 December 1941:

Geheime Kommandosache (classified message)

The 216.InfDiv will be transported via rail to *Heeresgruppe* [HG – Army Group] *Mitte* [Centre]. Upon arrival it will be attached to HG *Mitte*. *Oberkommando* [supreme command] will instruct *Feldtransport-Abteilung* [transport battalion] that each 5cm PaK is to be hauled by tractor to the division to reinforce its PzJgAbt. Each company will receive sufficient 5cm PaK to equip one platoon.

In January 1941, the normal provision of 3.7cm PaK for a *Panzerjäger-Abteilung* (PzJgAbt – anti-tank battalion) was 36 in three companies. Furthermore, the three infantry regiments each had an anti-tank company equipped with 12 of the type; a total of 72 guns. These companies were organized according to *Kriegstärkenachweisung* (KStN – table of organization) 184(c) or (d).

Since production of 5cm PaK 38 was not sufficient to re-equip all units, a number of *Teileinheit* (subunit) structures were created. This allowed a small number of the guns to be issued to reinforce the tank destroyer companies equipped with the 3.7cm PaK.

The first table of organization, KStN 188c, for the *Infanterie-Panzerjager-Zug Geschütz* 5cm (mot Z) (TE) (InfPzJgZg – infantry anti-tank gun platoon two 5cm guns motor traction) was published in January 1941. A month later the structure was complemented or replaced by KStN 215.

InfPzJgZg 2

This replaced the 4./*Zug* (platoon) of a regular 3.7cm PaK-armed InfPzJgKp. The first to be affected were those in Panzer divisions and motorized infantry divisions; standard infantry divisions were treated less favourably.

For newly established units a further structure, KStN 1142, was introduced which referred to a PzJgKp 'C' equipped with eight 3.7cm PaK and three 5cm PaK 38.

Although the introduction of the 5cm PaK 38 gave more fire power, weapon mobility was a problem. Whereas the 3.7cm PaK (435kg) could be handled by the four-man crew over most terrain, the heavier (900kg) PaK

38 – despite being fitted with castor wheels – was almost impossible for the crew to manoeuvre. Subsequently, motor vehicles or half-track tractors were an absolute requirement. However, since the availability of a suitable tractor was never a certainty, particularly in the mud season or winter, a team of heavy horses would be used.

Mobility would be a constant problem for all towed anti-tank units up until end of the war in 1945.

A document dated April 1942, distributed by *Armeeoberkommando* (AOK – Army High Command) 18 reveals:

Oberkommando des Heeres, (OKH – army high command) has confirmed the reinforcement of tank destroyer units with heavy armour-piercing weapons as stated in the order dated 9 March 1942.

II. Provision with 7.62cm PaK (mot Z)

1) It is expected that the army will receive 7.62cm PaK (mot Z) at the beginning of May, and two guns will be issued to platoons in each to PzJgAbt in an InfDiv and InfDiv (mot). The first target is to re-equip one platoon which has four 3.7cm PaK with two 7.62cm PaK.

2) The army has determined the sequence:
21.InfDiv, 96.InfDiv, 269.InfDiv, 11.InfDiv, 121.InfDiv, 254.InfDiv, 291.InfDiv, 1.InfDiv, 227.InfDiv, 61.InfDiv, 215.InfDiv, 58.InfDiv, 126. InfDiv, 217.InfDiv, 212.InfDiv and 224.InfDiv. Also 20.InfDiv (mot) and SS-Polizei-Division.

3) KStN are not yet available, but will be provided later. OKH is urgently proceeding with the procurement of suitable foreign-built [captured] towing tractors. If this is not possible, all divisions will have to improvise by using any available vehicle. As a final resort, teams of horses will have to be utilized.

4) ...

5) After the first units have been supplied, it is planned for the gradual re-equipment to continue.

III. Target for the supply of 5cm PaK 38

As more PaK 38 become available, the next target will be the gradual re-equipping of PzJg and InfPzJg units:

1. Infantry divisions
   a) PzJgKp in InfRgt   Two Zug: four PaK 38
                                 Two Zug: six 3.7cm PaK

Far left: The terrain and weather condition caused many anti-tank units in Russia to mount a weapon on a half-track tractor. Here men from PzJgAbt 13 (13.PzDiv) have mounted a gun and stabilized it with some wooden beams. Field engineers have fitted armour plates on the front of the vehicle to protect the engine radiator and fabricated a small travel rest to prevent the 5cm PaK 38 from being damaged.

b) PzJgKp in PzJgAbt	One Zug: two heavy PaK
	Two Zug: eight 3.7cm PaK
2. Panzer divisions	
SchtzRgt and KradSchtzBtl	All Zug: one PaK 38 each
	Later the PzJgZg of the SchtzBtl will also replace the three 3.7cm PaK with three PaK 38
3. Infantry divisions (mot)	
a) PzJgZg in InfRgt and	All Zug: three PaK 38
KradSchtzBtl	
b) PzJgZg in InfBtl	All Zug: will retain 3.7cm PaK
c) Kp in PzJgAbt	Two Zug: six PaK 38 or
	One Zug: three PaK 38 and
	One Zug: two 7.62cm PaK 36

On 10 May, AOK 18 reported that the delivery of 90 7.62cm PaK 36 were expected by the end of July. All remaining 7.62cm FK(r), without a re-bored breech chamber, were to be returned to AOK 18.

The supply of suitable tractor units remained a great problem. Item 3 in the above document refers to 60 French-built Somua half-track tractors, but the vehicle was unsuitable for towing heavy anti-tank guns. Consequently, all units were ordered to use them very carefully.

Advanced SP Anti-tank Weapons

Before the outbreak World War II, the HWA had demanded the design and development of *Selbstfahrlafette* (Sfl – self-propelled [SP]) guns for the artillery and self-propelled tank destroyers. But due to financial constraints, the shortage of materials and lack of production facilities, these demands went unheeded.

Self-propelled guns were in principle an effective method of rapidly deploying firepower. However, there were a number of disadvantages; most types lacked armour protection for the crew and were fitted with a conspicuous superstructure. This made the type a prime target for enemy gunners. Once again, the German army could not be supplied with the best possible equipment: it was not even possible to develop a dedicated chassis and running gear for a self-propelled gun; instead those of obsolete types had to be modified and utilized.

The first type of self-propelled anti-tank gun, a 4.7cm PaK(t) mounted on the chassis of PzKpfw I light tank, entered service in 1940. A total of 202

vehicles were produced, but the type was underpowered and mechanically unreliable and could only defeat a tank with thin armour.

In preparation for the forthcoming *Unternehmen* Barbarossa, military planners decided to produce 200 self-propelled anti-tank guns by mounting a 4.7cm PaK(t) on the chassis of captured French R-35 light tanks. The vehicles were delivered to three independent PzJgAbt, but after devastating losses all were transported to France and delivered to garrison units.

One of the many Universal Carriers abandoned, in working order, by British forces as they retreated to Dunkirk. German engineers have mounted an Austrian-built 47mm Böhler to realize a somewhat rudimentary self-propelled anti-tank gun.

The 7.5cm PaK 97/98 was mounted on the chassis of a number of T-26 tanks captured from Russian forces. In September 1943, 3.Kp in PzJgAbt 563, an independent (army group), was reported as having five of these self-propelled guns in its inventory.

It soon became obvious that a more powerful self-propelled anti-tank gun would be required to defeat the Soviet-built T-34 and KV tank. Surprisingly, the first gun available was the 7.62cm PaK 36(r) which had been captured in substantial numbers as the Red Army retreated.

Military planners had become aware of the fact that the tank production would never be sufficient to fulfil the needs of Panzer and other front-line forces and ordered the development of self-propelled guns to be expedited. But again, due to the prevailing conditions in the Reich, they were forced to use the chassis of outdated types.

PzSfl 1 for 7.62cm PaK 36

Some years before the war, MAN had developed a tank for the light divisions. The PzKpfw II Ausf D was capable of travelling at 55kph; higher than the speed of a standard PzKpfw II. For several reasons the type was cancelled, but it was developed as a special infantry support tank; the PzKpfw II *Flammpanzer* (Fl – flame-thrower tank). On 7 December 1941, the *Organisationsabteilung* (OrgAbt – organization battalion) decreed that the planned second batch of *Flammpanzer* tanks was to be cancelled and the chassis used as the basis for an armoured self-propelled *Panzerjäger*. The conversion would be reasonably simple: After removing the turret, a T-shaped *Grundplatte* (base plate) was bolted to the strengthened superstructure before mounting the upper gun carriage. To offer some protection for the crew, a simple armoured (14.5mm [front] and 10mm [side]) superstructure was fitted. Designated PzSfl 1 für 7.62cm PaK 36(r), production ended after 150 had been converted.

PzSfl 2 for 7.62cm PaK 36

A second self-propelled *Panzerjäger* was being developed at the same time as the above type. At the end of 1941, the Czech-built PzKpfw 38(t) was still in service with some Panzer divisions despite being outdated, However, the type had proven to be a mechanically rugged and reliable performer on the battlefield. Military planners decided that it was the obvious choice for conversion.

Firstly, a percentage of complete PzKpfw 38(t) chassis were diverted from the running production lines for alterations. A base plate, on which the PaK 36 was mounted, was produced and fitted over the fighting compartment. The simple superstructure, to protect the crew, was fabricated from thin

When France capitulated a large number of Lorraine 37L supply tractors were captured. German engineers soon identified the versatile vehicle as being suitable for conversion as a self-propelled gun carrier. One such vehicle was the 7.5cm PaK 40/1 *auf Geschutzwagen-Lorraine-Schlepper* (f), known as the Marder I. Production of the 37L continued in Vichy-controlled France until 1945.

The extra weight of the gun mounting and protective armour was acknowledged as being the cause of the Marder I being mechanically unreliable. In April 1943, German military officials decided to send any surviving vehicles to units in France and replaced it with the Marder III.

armour plate: A small gun shield he was also fitted. The self-propelled gun was designated PzSfl 2 für 7.62cm PaK 36 and between April and October 1942, some 344 were produced.

With availability of 7.5cm PaK 40, planners decided that this was the gun to be mounted on all future conversions..

PzJg Lorraine for 7.5cm PaK 40/1: Marder I

The German military also examined various types of captured vehicles to evaluate if any were suitable for conversion to an SP gun. During the rapid invasion of France in 1940, a significant number of abandoned but serviceable British and French tanks and other vehicles were captured. One was the fully-tracked Lorraine 37L, *Tracteur de Revitaillement pour Chars* 1937L (supply tractor 1937L), which was thought to be suitable and under the supervision of Major Becker – a capable engineer who had established a command in France and went on to produce a number of SP guns on a captured chassis. Becker obtained a 37L chassis, which had a a centre-mounted engine, and began conversion work having already decided to arm the type with a 7.5cm PaK 40. By late June, the prototype had been completed and then sent to Germany for appraisal by Adolf Hitler. He was impressed and gave his approval for the type to go into production. Fabrication of parts for the superstructure was carried by Alkett; these were then shipped to *Heeres-Kraftfahrpark* (HKP – army vehicle park) in Paris (and Bielitz) where facilities had been established to assemble the SP guns. A sensible move given the prevailing state of the German armaments industry.

The *Marder* (Marten) I entered service between July and August 1942 and a total of 170 were completed.

PzJg II for 7.5cm PaK 40/2: Marder II

In May 1942, studies revealed that the hull of a PzKpfw II was suitable for conversion as a 7.5cm *Panzerjäger*, since it required little modification. Alkett was selected to carry out the work and managed to deliver a prototype by June. After a series of trials, the type was accepted and ordered into mass production using refurbished PzKpfw chassis. Since supply of these guns could not match the demand, orders were given for complete PzKpfw II to be diverted from the production line and converted. Such was the demand that vehicle manufacturers Ursus and Famo were also contracted.

By 1942 the *Panzerjäger* I had long been considered as obsolete; many of the type had been in service since the mid-1930s and despite receiving regular maintenance had become mechanically unreliable. Although the Czech-built 4.7cm PaK(t) lacked performance, against the latest enemy armour a number of PzJg I remained in service with German forces in North Africa and Russia until 1943.

By early 1943, a total of 533 Marder II had been delivered when production ended. The type was replaced in service by the Marder 38 built using a PzKpfw 38(t) chassis. At the same time, Ursus and Famo were contracted to build the *Wespe* (wasp) self-propelled artillery gun.

PzJg 38 for 7.5cm PaK 40/3: Marder 38

In mid-1942, military planners decided that all Panzer divisions operating the Czech-built PzKpfw 38(t) would be re-equipped with German-built tanks to increase the number of chassis for conversion. This is confirmed by an entry in the *Kriegstagebuch* (KTB – war diary) of the OKH which notes that all production capacity at Bömisch-Märische-Maschinenfabrik (BMM) was to be utilized to build the type.

When PzSfl 2 production ended, work had begun on the design and development of an improved SP gun, mounting a 7.5cm PaK 40/3. The design was straightforward, since it utilized an almost unchanged PzKpfw 38(t) hull and running gear. The fighting compartment was plated over and a *Trägerplatte* (carrier plate) was fitted to mount the slightly modified gun.

As more 7.5cm PaK 40 guns became available, military planners decided that the PzKpfw II chassis should be utilized for the production of a self-propelled gun. The Bosch headlamp identifies this as a late production vehicle.

A simple armoured superstructure was fitted which gave limited protection to the gun crew. A total of 275 Marder 38 were produced between November 1942 and May 1943, many being built on refurbished PzKpfw 38(t) hulls.

In early 1943, BMM had completed development of the *Geschützwagen* (GW – gun carrier) 38, an improved type which was designed to mount different and also heavier guns. The major change made by BMM engineers was to move the engine forward to create a more spacious fighting compartment with easier access for the crew.

For clarity the new version was designated Marder 38 Ausf M or *Panzerjäger* 38 Ausf M, whereas the earlier type was re-designated the Ausf H. The type was also known as the Marder III. A total of 942 had been built by 1945.

Organization

When available, self-propelled tank destroyers were issued to *Panzerjäger-Kompanien* (PzJgKp – tank destroyer company) and *Panzerjäger-Abteilungen*

When compared to the PzSfl I and PzSfl II, the Marder II had a larger fighting compartment and much better protection for the crew, but only had room for 37 rounds of 7.5cm GrPatr ammunition.

The French-built *Canon de 47mm semi-automatique Mle* 1937 was followed, two years later, by an improved model 1939. Those which survived the Battle of France were taken into German service: the model 1937 was designated 4.7cm PaK 181(f) and the model 1939 as the 4.7cm PaK 183(f). The weapon had a performance comparable to that of the 5cm PaK 38.

(tank destroyer battalion) in infantry and Panzer divisions. At the same time a number of independent PzJgAbt were established and armed with SP guns.

All available KStN were adapted and rewritten. In February 1942, KStN 1148 was used as the basic organization table for the new self-propelled *Panzerjäger* (Sfl) units; KStN 1148a listed a PzJgKp having nine SP guns and KStN 1149a shows that a *Teileinheit Panzerjäger-Zug* (PzJgZg – tank destroyer platoon) was to be issued with three SP guns.

Unfortunately the original KStN documents could not be found, since it was common practice for outdated KStN to be destroyed when a new version was issued.

After-action Report

The dynamic developments during 1942 are portrayed by a questionnaire for battalions. It was submitted by VII.*Armeekorps* and dealt with the fighting in the southern sector in July 1942. Excerpts read:

> Question:
> Are there any changes concerning the enemy tank's characteristics and armour protection?
> Answer:
> The frontal armour on the KV-1 has been reinforced with 5cm plates.

In mid-1942, the *Panzerjäger* began to receive deliveries of the 7.5cm PaK 40 and now had a weapon that could defeat the T-34 and KV tanks being deployed on the battlefront. The weapon was also used as a tank gun; the PzKpfw IV Ausf F2 and the Ausf G mounted a 7.5cm KwK 40. Another version; the 7.5cm StuK 40 was mounted in the *Sturmgeschutz*.

A new version of the T-34 with two turret hatches was encountered. One was destroyed south of Warnen [Oserki].

Question:

Is there anything to say about strengths and shortcomings of the newly engaged British-built Infantry Tank Mk II [Matilda II]?

Answer:

The Mk II is fabricated from high-grade steel, is fitted with excellent optics and the type is highly manoeuvrable. The glacis armour was seldomly penetrated by 7.5cm s PaK. The tank should be engaged from the sides.

Question:

How did the different ammunition types perform?

Answer:

The 7.5cm PzGrPatr 39 destroyed nearly all heavy tanks (Mk II [Matilda], T-34 and KV-1) at ranges up to 1,200m, at good angle of impact even at 1,600m. The penetration force of the Russian 7.62cm PaK is identical, but the HL round of the 7.5cm PaK 97/38 (ex-French) shows inferior performances, it could be used at ranges up to a maximum of 900m. A reinforced KV-1 could not be destroyed even after 19 hits at the side (when the drive sprocket was shot off, the crew bailed out). The PzGr 40 of the 5cm PaK 38 penetrated turret and rear of the KV-1 model 1942, but only at a range of 80m, even at favourable angle on impact. The PzGr 39 did not show any effect. HE rounds showed good results against infantry targets.

Question:

Are there any basic prerequisites for anti-tank defence?

Answer:

Extreme fire discipline is necessary when firing at long ranges, as are an effective camouflage and great graduation of the guns in the depth of the terrain. Reverse slope positions always proved to be advisable. The PaK 97/38 had good success when used flanking from shallow recesses.

The 7.5cm PaK 40 with its great effective range shows particular results: on two days each seven tanks were destroyed at 1,400m. On this occasion the only tanks engaged were those that had detected our anti-tank positions. But the smoke and dust created could not be concealed and quickly attracted the attention of enemy artillery. This also affected our ability to maintain visual contact with the tanks.

Question:

What manner of coordinating our anti-tank weapons worked best?

Answer:

Creation of combat groups (engineers with magnetic mines and infantry) was essential to protect the foremost s PaK. To avoid a flanking attack all guns have to be emplaced in positions able to guard and protect each other. A triangular positioning proved to be favourable. If possible, cooperation with 8.8cm FlaK deployed farther in the rear is advisable. Due to their great range the AA guns can have effect far in front of our anti-tank guns.

The Marder II, like most self-propelled guns of the time, simply utilized a standard tank chassis fitted with an inevitably high superstructure. Many commanders appreciated its mobility, but also complained that the vehicle was difficult to conceal.

Question:

How did the high-explosive round perform?

Answer:

As mentioned above, high-explosive (HE) rounds had good effect against infantry targets. As yet we have not engaged enemy tanks with HE rounds.

Question:

What were the armour-piercing capabilities of our weapons?

Answer:

The PzGr 39 fired by the s PaK showed much better armour-piercing capability than stated in the official instructional pamphlet.

Question:

Further experiences?

Answer:

It is absolutely necessary to provide each gun with two magnetic mines. For moving in position in the course of own rolling tank assaults low cross-country tractors are indispensible. Opel Allrad [four-wheel-drive 3-ton truck] and Unik [French-built Unic P107 half-track tractor] have proven to be inappropriate, since they will be spotted and engaged easily. The tractors must be spacious to transport the crew with gear and ammunition. Each platoon must be issued with at least one heavy motorcycle with sidecar. Using the small motorcycles the platoon leaders could lead their guns unharmed, since they were often not noticed by moving tanks. The wheels of the PaK 97/38 should be wider to prevent them sinking into wet ground.

Experiences and deficiencies:

1) 7.5cm PaK 40

The lead device will generally not be used. Aiming with the main notch is generally sufficient and allows a quicker rate of fire. Jammed cartridges were a frequent problem. A small trench must be dug in front of the gun to operate the cleaning rod. A remedy is absolute necessary. The equilibrator tends to leak frequently. A better sealing is necessary. We improved on things by replacing the high-temperature oil with standard gear oil.

2) 7.62cm PaK (Russian)

Concerning effectiveness and penetration force the gun is identical to the German 7.5cm PaK 40. Due to its simple armour shield the gun is lighter than the PaK 40. [Note, This statement is wrong, both PaK 36 and PaK 39 were heavier than the PaK 40. It is however possible that the pneumatic tyres made movement easier.] The gun's great height is disadvantageous. Jamming cartridges were not encountered so far.

3) 7.5cm PaK 97/38(f)

Clear penetrations (engaging heavy tanks) are possible at ranges below 800m. The simple breech eased the gun's operation [The French-built gun had no sliding breech block, but an interrupter screw-type breech]. After firing, the barrel frequently remained in the rear position because the pneumatic pressure in the recuperator was too low. The troop cannot refill the system. The tyres are too narrow on soft ground. It is impossible to pivot the gun manually. The manual firing is too susceptible, shots can be unloaded unintentionally.

4) 5cm PaK 38

The PaK shows only low penetration even at near ranges and when using PzGr 40. The side traverse gear tends to soil easily. A better cover for the sector gear is desirable. The hand wheel for the traversing gear jams frequently. A grease point would solve the problem.

Summarizing we suggest to issue only 7.5cm PaK guns.

A Marder II being driven to the battlefront over ground covered by the first snow of winter. Although roomier than other self-propelled guns, food and the crew's personal belongings were stowed in a carrier mounted on the rear of the vehicle.

Panzerarmee Afrika 2

On 30 November 1941, British forces in North Africa succeeded in breaking out of their defensive positions, especially from those around Tobruk. German forces were forced to retreat, but managed to regroup and launch a number of counterattacks.

In early 1942, the *Luftwaffe* had virtually neutralized the air defences of Malta, and this allowed German transport aircraft and Axis shipping to supply Rommel with fuel, food, fighting vehicles and troop reinforcements. The revitalized *Panzerarmee Afrika* (Tank Army Africa) attacked on several fronts and pushed the British forces back to El Alamein.

But German anti-tank defence in North Africa was at the limits of its effectiveness. The 3.7cm PaK 36 could not be used to defeat the more heavily armoured British tanks, but many units deployed the gun as a multi-purpose support weapon.

By late 1941, the 5cm PaK 38 had become the standard anti-tank weapon in service with German forces fighting in the desert. At ranges of 350m to 500m, when firing PzGr 40 ammunition, the gun was effective against most British tanks; only the Infantry Tank Mark II Matilda was difficult to defeat. At ranges above 500m, the highly effective 8.8cm FlaK would be called into action.

Towed anti-tank guns were in return most vulnerable to high-explosive (HE) fire but fortunately the majority of British tanks – Cruiser Tank Mark I to Mark IV – were armed with the Ordnance QF 2 Pounder. High-explosive ammunition for the gun was in development and unavailable, which made it almost impossible to knock-out a well dug-in German anti-tank gun.

The *Panzerjäger* I was the first self-propelled tank destroyer to be produced for the German military. The type utilized a Pzkpfw I Ausf B chassis and mounted a Škoda-built 47mm gun fitted with a high defensive shield. The weapon, when firing PzGr 40 ammunition, could defeat a British Infantry Tank Mk II 'Matilda' at a range of 400m.

The 76mm divisional gun M1936 entered service with Red Army as a semi-universal (including anti-aircraft defence) gun. Vast numbers were abandoned by retreating Soviet forces in the first months of *Unternehmen* Barbarossa and captured by German units. The type was designated 7.62cm FK 296(r).

Troops fighting on the Eastern Front, demanded a new anti-tank weapon. As a simple expedient, military planners ordered the delivery of captured Soviet-built 76.2mm field guns. On 21 December 1941, the OrgAbt confirmed that 60 of these field guns had been delivered to *Panzergruppe Afrika*. Designated as 7.62cm *Feldkanone* (FK – field gun) 296(r), the guns were delivered complete with a plentiful supply of original Soviet ammunition. The gun had an effective high muzzle velocity, and could defeat a Matilda II at ranges of 600 to 800m.

An entry in the war diary of OrgAbt dated 25 January 1942 stated:

The Führer orders the immediate replacement in full of the losses suffered by *Panzerarmee Afrika*. An extra 10 per cent in the number of tanks required shall be issued. A respective order will be issued to *Befehlshaber des Ersatzheeres* [BdE – commander of the replacement training army]. At the same time all units are requested to submit reports on any new British weapons, US Army tanks and the performance of German weapons.

Panzerarmee Afrika responded that as yet no new types of British tanks or anti-tank weapons have been encountered. So far only one US Army tank has been captured intact. An exact technical description and the results of firing trials will be provided later.

Our anti-tank weapons have proven most effective during the fighting, especially the 5cm PaK 38 and *Kampfwagenkanone* (KwK – tank gun) are clearly superior.

The 7.62cm FK 296(r) anti-tank guns delivered to 15.PzDiv, 21.PzDiv, and also 90.le Afrika Division were quickly adopted by the troops and used on the battlefront.

The war diary of 90.le Afrika Division contains a mysterious after-action report, dated 25 March 1942. It was written by the commander of *Kampfgruppe* Tmimi, an ad hoc task force established on the orders of the division commander:

Statement on the loss of strongpoint 'Käthe', 21 March 1942

1) Immediately after assuming command of 'Käthe' I was ordered to reinforce the strongpoint with heavy weapons because the enemy had made repeated attacks over the preceding days. At the time the following weapons were at hand: Five light *Machinengewehr* [MG – machine gun], a heavy MG, two heavy *Granatwerfer* [GrWrf – mortar], one 3.7cm PaK, one PzB 41 (issued by MG-Battalion 5). I then commandeered the following from *Kampfgruppe* [combat group] Tmimi: Five *Russen-Geschütze* [Russian guns], two PzB 41, two heavy GrWrf, 11 light MG.

The breech block and gun sight of a 7.62cm FK 296(r), originally produced as a divisional gun for the Red Army, it did not have a telescope-type gun sight. But his was rectified when the weapon was re-chambered to accept German ammunition and a *Zielfernrohr* (sighting telescope) was fitted.

2) At 06:46hrs on 21 March, I was informed that 'Käthe' was target of a heavy attack by 400 enemy infantry from the west and supported by two artillery batteries from south. Armoured vehicles were initially not reported and I was informed of enemy tanks only after the fall of 'Käthe', but it was too late to intervene. Position 'Käthe' was well equipped with heavy weapons which made such a quick defeat unlikely. The attacks today replicated those of the previous days, which we repelled with some ease. By 08:30hrs, positions 'Anna' and 'Gerda' simultaneously reported heavy attacks on their strongpoints. It is known that 'Käthe' had sent radio messages complaining of the lack of supporting artillery fire. I immediately attempted to contact the *Artillerie-Führer* [artillery commander] Major Gräf and was informed that he had been replaced earlier. I personally intervened and instructed the new commander, Hauptmann Unrau, to immediately provide artillery support for positions 'Anna' and 'Gerda'.
I made repeated attempts to contact the commander of II./PzArtRgt 33 but he could not be reached. The discharge of Major Gräf was not reported to me nor to the replacement commander. At 09.40hrs, I decided to go to the forward command post on Tmimi Heights in order to gain a clear view of the situation. I informed my division continuously as to the situation. Since my offer to send reconnaissance units was rejected, I requested air reconnaissance to prepare for bombing enemy positions. The latter was also rejected, since our aircraft could not fly due to the runway being waterlogged. I am convinced that an air raid would have changed the situation at 'Käthe'.

3) A final assessment of the reasons for the fall of 'Käthe' is not possible, since no survivors could be found. I am sure that the defeat was caused by a sequence of unfortunate circumstances:

a) The lack of supporting artillery fire caused by the incorrect implementation of the order to dismiss Major Gräf.

b) The refusal to allow any reconnaissance.

c) The 7.62cm *Russen-Geschütze* (Russian 7.62cm FK 296[r]) did not meet the expectations against enemy armour.

4) ...

5) The fact we found more than 100 spent shell cases indicates that position 'Käthe' had not been given up without fight. However, we suspect that our FK 296 guns were not dug-in but were in open positions. The speed and ferocity of enemy tank assault was such that the guns had no chance to target accurately.

6) The combat value of the Russian guns against tanks might be not as good as expected, as it is quite heavy, making it very difficult for the crew to manoeuvre. One serious problem is that the Gunner 1 cannot easily fire the gun; indeed the trigger is located near Gunner 2. Even more problematic; the traversing and elevating wheels are not positioned close together on the same side as the

gunner and have to be operated by two men. The gunsight must be kept on enemy tanks – even if they zig-zag – as they attack, but due to the above this results in a fatal loss of time. As the gun is fired, both Gunner 1 and Gunner 2 have to jump back from their positions to avoid the long recoil. Another problem is that the gunsight is mounted too high, so that a small gunner has to stand on a wooden crate or similar to sight the weapon.

The exact type of ammunition used at 'Käthe', and its effect during the battle, cannot be determined due to lack of survivors.

The main body of German forces had arrived in North Africa by 12 March 1941. Experience gained in the first months of battle identified an urgent requirement for an effective self-propelled anti-tank gun. The first became available in January 1942 when the 7.62cm PaK 36(r) was mounted on the SdKfz 6 medium half-track tractor.

Despite the fact that the very same strongpoint was attacked several times in the days beforehand, the British assault still took the German defenders by surprise.

After the battle the process of avoiding blame began, but the loss of some 400 men and a significant amount of precious equipment could not be overlooked. Tactically the German defenders had not prepared an effective defensive line and anti-tank guns were not dug in, but deployed in open positions and easily eliminated by enemy tank and artillery fire. A significant fact is that the well-led British forces struck without warning with a head-on attack supported by artillery fire from the opposite direction. The absence of artillery support from German batteries could only have aggravated the dire situation faced by the defenders.

German gun crews experienced numerous problems operating the 7.62cm FK 296(r); this is not surprising since the weapon was developed as a field gun,

Despite being outdated, the *Panzerbüchse* (PzB – anti-tank rifle) 39 was still in front-line use in 1942 and not declared obsolete until late 1944. It was fitted with a Mauser-type breech mechanism and two magazines, each containing ten rounds, which could be attached to each side of the weapon.

not an anti-tank gun. The FK 296(r) was cumbersome and slow to operate, which was exacerbated by a lack of sufficient training before combat: Only a well-drilled crew could use the gun effectively.

On 24 April, the commander of 90.le AfrikaDiv was informed by *Panzerarmee Afrika* that 96 FK 296(r) would be delivered to reinforce his infantry regiments, but the number of suitable tractors could not be ensured. The division reported that it had 59 suitable tractors available, along with a number of SdKfz 10, some four-wheel drive trucks and a large number of captured vehicles.

The usage of railway trucks was not possible since that would weaken the delivery of vital supplies. The commander then emphasized the need for the extra 37 tractors.

Also on the same day, 90.le AfrikaDiv reported that the following heavy weapons were operational. At that time two tank destroyer battalions – PzJgAbt 190 and 605 – were attached to the division:

PaK 36 (7.62cm)	- 58
PzSfl 2 (7.62cm PaK Sfl)	- Two
PzJg I (4.7cm PaK Sfl)	- 13
le FH 18	- Two
lePzB 38	- Two
sPzB 41	- 12

However, these numbers changed constantly due to heavy losses in combat.

Later combat availability reports prove that the Soviet-built 7.62cm was numerically the most important anti-tank gun. Artillery units especially relied on this gun, since it had better anti-tank performance than a leFH 18.

But warfare in North Africa for German forces was characterized by ever-present shortages. A lack of prime movers (half-track tractors and four-wheel drive trucks) meant that weapons could not be moved and any vehicles commandeered from other units would only cause more problems. In an attempt to make up the shortage, German forces utilized every captured, or found abandoned, British vehicle or repaired those which had been disabled.

Combat availability reports show that the German artillery and anti-tank units were not uniformly equipped and could have German guns, Russian-built guns and when available guns captured from the British; some units even used Italian guns. In fact PzJgAbt 605, the tank destroyer unit in 90.leDiv, is known to have used captured British tanks.

In March 1943, 90.leDiv was in the process of being reorganized as a PzGrDiv. A Panzer battalion (PzAbt 190) was formed with an integral PzJgAbt of two platoons. It was intended that each would be equipped with ten PzSfl 2 (7.62cm PaK 36 Sfl), but seven had been lost in battle during the preceding two months.

In preparation for *Unternehmen* Theseus – the advance on Tobruk – OKH decided to order the delivery of six 7.62cm(r) Sfl (PzSfl 2) to *Panzerarmee Afrika*; a further six were to be delivered at a later date.

On 24 June 1942, four days after German forces captured Tobruk, *Oberkommmando der Panzerarmee Afrika* reported:

1) The mood and morale of our troops is outstanding, despite the tense situation.

2)...

3) Supply situation:

Sufficient stocks are available in all areas of supply, but with the exception of a few types of ammunition.

Approximately 80 tanks are operational, but a significant number of tractors have been destroyed. The lack of supply trucks is extremely worrying.

4) We request:
  a) 60: PaK 38
     80: 3.7cm PaK
     Ten: leFh
     Eight: 10cm Kanonen
  b) A more constant supply of PzKpfw III and PzKpfw IV. The same applies
     for the 5cm PaK. There is also a requirement for 50 half-track vehicles of
     all types.

It seems that the *Panzerarmee* was not interested in receiving heavy anti-tank
weapons, such as the 7.62cm PaK 36 or the self-propelled tank destroyer, but
requested delivery of the 5cm PaK 38 and the 'outdated' 3.7cm PaK. Possibly
this was due to the fast-moving nature of the fighting in North Africa where
all anti-tank units had to keep pace with the tank force.

In July 1942, the German advance had been halted and *Panzerarmee Afrika*
reported that Axis forces were now fighting defensively. The strength figures
had fallen drastically:

Troops: 30 per cent of target
Tanks: 15 per cent of target
Artillery: 70 per cent of target
PaK: 40 per cent of target
Heavy FlaK: 50 per cent of target

On 21 July 1942, all German units involved delivered their strength reports:
  15. PzDiv

PzRgt 8	Four PzKpfw II, 14 PzKpfw III
PzGrenRgt 115	Six 5cm PaK; three 5.7cm PaK Sfl (British),
	Six field guns; eight 76cm (British)
PzArtRgt 33	19 leFH; five s FH; one 10cm Kanone
PzJgAbt 33	Eight 5cm PaK; one 4cm Sfl (British)
PzPiBtl 33	Two 5cm PaK

  21. PzDiv

PzRgt 5	Five PzKpfw III; 14 PzKpfw III (Special)
PzGrenRgt 104	11 5cm PaK; five 4cm PaK (British);
	four 5.7cm PaK (British); two 7.62cm PaK (Russian);
	three 8.76cm field guns (British)

PzArtRgt 33	14 leFH; six sFH; three 10cm Kanone, four 8.76cm field guns (British)
PzJgAbt 33	Nine 5cm PaK

German forces had captured an astonishing amount of British equipment, including a significant number of the Ordnance Quick-Firing (QF) 25 Pounder [8.76cm] field gun and howitzer. Also captured were a number of AEC-built Mk I Gun Carrier, 'Deacon' which mounted an Ordnance QF 6-Pounder [5.7cm] anti-tank gun.

In August 1942, the situation had again changed as more supplies reached the *Panzerarmee*, due to an increased number of Axis ships and transport aircraft getting through unhindered. The number of tanks available was 50 per cent of the target and the number of anti-tank weapons was 60 per cent of the target.

In this situation Rommel decided that he now had sufficient equipment to continue the advance. However, Royal Air Force squadrons on Malta, which had been re-equipped and strengthened, began to intensify attacks on Axis shipping and air transport.

The 2.8cm *schwerer Panzerbüchse* (s PzB – heavy anti-tank rifle) 41 was never popular with anti-tank teams fighting in North Africa. The weapon had outstanding performance against enemy armour at below 500m, but as the range increased effectiveness and accuracy rapidly diminished.

On 2 September 1942, *Panzerarmee Afrika* sent an alarming message by teletype:

The absence of the required quantity of fuel [and other supplies] makes the continuation of the assault impossible.

At present the fuel situation is as follows: In our territory we have three *Verbrauchsatz* [VS – fuel consumption data] available, but supply is guaranteed only until 5 September. In the recent days 2,610t of fuel was delivered, a further 3,352t was lost at sea. Some 443t of ammunition was delivered, but 350t was lost at sea.

The 8.8cm *Flugzeugabwehrkanone* (FlaK – anti-aircraft gun) was also an effective anti-tank weapon and much feared by the crews of British and Commonwealth armoured units.

The message underlines the strategic importance of 'aircraft carrier' Malta. Although an invasion plan was prepared, German supreme command came to the conclusion that occupation was unnecessary; historically a serious misjudgment.

By mid-1942 the threat level in North Africa had changed. The Allied troops were issued with great number of the US-built M3 Medium tank.

The command echelon of *Deutsches Afrika Korps* reported:

A 7.62cm FK(r) *auf gepanzerte Selbstfahrlafette* was purpose-built to fill a desperate shortage of self-propelled guns in North Africa. The type utilized the chassis of an SdKfz 6 medium tractor, and was fitted with a simple box-like superstructure, to protect the gun and crew. The gun could defeat any British tank, but the type was very conspicuous on the battlefield, often falling victim to artillery or ground-attack aircraft.

After-action reports regarding the fighting from May to June 1942:

A) Enemy tactics and fighting

II.) Single weapons
1.) Tanks
Each attack by the enemy is supported by a heavy artillery barrage. If this proves to be ineffective, then the 7.5cm gun of the 'Pilot' is used. We could not verify any cooperation with anti-tank weapons. The flanks of the attack were protected by SP guns.

Contrary to earlier battles, heavy fire from machine guns was effectively used. This restricted action by our anti-tank guns, disrupted refuelling and also ammunition being replenished. The enemy seriously fears our PaK, also the 8.8cm FlaK and the PzKpfw IV. We did not encounter any British Mk IV, V or VI tanks.

4.) Anti-tank defence
The new British 5.7cm anti-tank gun [QF 6-Pounder] and the 7.5cm [75mm Gun M2/M3] mounted in the 'Pilot' have a superior effective firing range over our 5cm PaK. This has led to heavy losses in our tank destroyer companies, despite the fact that the 5.7cm anti-tank gun only fired armour-piercing rounds.

[Note: 'Pilot' was the name German forces used to identify the US-built M3 General Lee or Grant medium tank. The self-propelled guns mentioned are probably the AEC Deacon.]

The German 5cm PaK was apparently effective against most British tanks. This superiority applied all the more to the 7.62cm FK 296(r) and PaK 36 and the 8.8cm FlaK. Until mid-1942 British tank assaults lacked a tank firing effective high-explosive ammunition and German anti-tank gun positions could effectively resist such attacks. For this reason the M3 medium was warmly welcomed, becoming a threat for the *Afrika Korps*.

With more M3 being available, FlaK-Rgt 135 reported the following experiences on 10 August 1942:

Commitment of *schwere Flugzeugabwehrkanone* [s FlaK – heavy anti-aircraft (AA) guns] with *Panzerbegleit-Batterien* [escort batteries].

Combat deployment must be changed. The gun can destroy a 'Pilot' at all combat ranges, but we must open fire much earlier at around 3,000m. The

Known as *Gigant* (giant), the Messerschmitt Me-323 had wings constructed from plywood and a fuselage built of metal tubing with wood formers; the entire airframe was covered with fabric. The nose of the aircraft opened as a pair of clam-shell doors for loading and unloading. Here *Luftwaffe* groundcrew load a 7.5cm PaK 40 into the cavernous cargo bay.

'Pilot' will open fire with its 7.5cm gun at around this range and the HE rounds are very effective against our 8.8cm. On numerous occasions our guns were forced to change position after having fired only a few rounds.

This report again underlines the importance of the M3 medium tank for Allied forces.

In August 1942 Major de Bouché, a *Verbindungsoffizier der Waffenamt* (liaison officer of the ordnance office), visited *Panzerarmee Afrika* with the task of collating a report on all weapons being used in North Africa. To gather the necessary information, he distributed a questionnaire to and also visited a significant number of front-line units. His final report was comprehensive and contained more than 30 pages.

In this supplement, the single weapons are dealt with according to the following parameters:

1) General troop assessment explaining usability in North Africa.
2) Technical/mechanical shortcomings.
3) Suggestions for improvement.

PzB 39

1) For modern warfare penetration performance is unsatisfactory. Units visited were no longer using this weapon.

2.8cm s PzB 41

1) The unanimous view is that the gun did not prove satisfactory, since its lacks effective combat range. Furthermore, the carriage is mechanically weak. The weapon is only effective against light armour of an armoured car or an SP gun. But before effective fire can be opened, the gun is often destroyed by long-range enemy weapons. Even when mounted on a truck, armoured halftrack or an armoured observation vehicle the gun proved ineffective.
2) The *Sonderanhänger* [SdAnh – special purpose trailer] 32 is not sturdy enough to carry the gun.
3) We suggest halting the supply of this weapon.

3.7cm PaK

1) Armour penetration is not sufficient for defeating a modern tank. It is not effective even against weakly armoured enemy tanks, since these will open fire at longer range with their 4cm [British QF 2 Pounder] gun before the 3.7cm PaK can.

The Me-323 was a six-engine military transport developed from the Me-321 heavy assault glider. The type had a cargo capacity of some 11,000kg, sufficient to transport an 8.8cm FlaK and its SdKfz 7 tractor. But it was slow and had a cruising speed of 218kph (135mph), so that many of those encountered were easily shot down by fighter aircraft; on one occasion by a B-26 Marauder bomber.

2) None.

3) Since the gun is clearly inferior to the British QF 2-Pounder gun, it must be rapidly replaced by the 5cm PaK 38.

4.2cm PaK 41

1) All 12 guns of the *Sonderverband* [SV – special task force] 288 were quickly lost due to enemy action. Although very effective at short range, the gun will be quickly defeated by longer-range enemy weapons.

2) The running gear is unsuited to the terrain, axles and suspension arms are easily broken. The ammunition is very effective, but is not available in sufficient amounts.

3) The guns must be replaced by the 5cm PaK 38.

4.7cm PaK(t) Sfl

1) The troops emphasize the excellent accuracy of this gun; up to a range of 1,000m the first round will be a hit. Regarding the special circumstances in the desert, the armour penetration is too weak. Of all small calibre weapons, the 4.7cm PaK is rated as the best.

2) When crossing the rock-strewn desert, the gun can be easily damaged. The firing trigger must be relocated to the elevating/traversing gear. The sighting telescope must be improved to a range of 4,000m. The transceiver radio lacks voice range since battery power is insufficient; the mounting rack is weak. The [PzKpfw I Ausf B] running gear is unreliable, leaf springs break frequently. The Maybach engine lacks power and easily overheats.

3) Rear armour protection should be improved, but this is not possible since it would increase vehicle weight.

5cm PaK 38

1) Armour penetration against all enemy tanks encountered is rated excellent at ranges up to 2,000m. If the sighting telescope was improved, enemy tanks could be engaged at ranges over 2,000m. The front-line troops demand that more be delivered.

2) Traversing the gun must be improved, the pivot is too weak. A stronger hollow type, as on the British 5.7cm [QF 6 Pounder] gun, must be introduced. The sighting telescope mounting is easily clogged with dust and this will affect operation. The trigger mechanism on the handwheel is too stiff and must be adjusted for smoother operation. Preferably, the trigger should be pushed forward to fire the gun. The grooved solid rubber tyres on the carriage wheels became jammed with stones which ripped them to pieces.

7.62cm PaK 36(r)

The penetration ability of both guns (standard and bored-out) is outstanding and sufficient to defeat most types of enemy tanks engaged. During firing trials with a bored-out gun, using German ammunition, the turret of a captured British Matilda II (9cm armour) was penetrated twice. If the sighting telescope was improved the gun could operate at ranges up to at least 4,000m. However, accuracy is not as good as the smaller calibre guns. The gun is feared by the enemy, and is always fiercely attacked when spotted on the battlefront. During the recent advance all guns were hit by enemy fire, leading to their temporary loss.

The gun is available in the following versions:

7.62cm FK 296(r) (standard) with few alterations as a towed anti-tank gun: The gun carriage is too weak for traversing desert terrain. Furthermore, the recoil causes the gun to move after firing. Consequently, the gun has to be re-aimed.

7.62cm FK 296(r) (standard) on SdKfz 6/3 as a self-propelled gun: The gunsight is poor and simply must be improved. The gunner must be able to pull the trigger as on our PaK; the trigger must be mounted adjacent to the setting mechanism and operated by pushing it forward. The profile of the

In May 1942, a total of 12 PzSfl 2 were delivered to North Africa and issued to 15.PzDiv and 21.PzDiv. The vehicle mounted a highly effective 7.62cm PaK 36(r) which gave German forces a very mobile anti-tank gun capable of defeating all British-built tanks.

vehicle is far too high, which makes it conspicuous. Armour protection is too weak and is easily penetrated by machine-gun fire. Also, the vehicle easily catches fire when hit. Despite being lightly armoured, the vehicle is far too slow: a faster chassis to mount a 7.62cm PaK must be given some priority. To lower the profile, the gun could be mounted facing to the rear and this would allow the gun to be traversed 90 degrees to both sides. A thicker gun shield is very important.

7.62cm PaK 36 (bored out), with muzzle brake as SP gun on Praga tank (PzSfl 2): The same firing problems as above. When secured in the travel lock, the

position of the gun barrel is too high; this together with a large muzzle brake makes a PzSfl 2 very conspicuous. A lower travel lock is necessary. The gun shield mounting brackets are weak too and constantly break. Operation of the traverse and elevating mechanism is too stiff; a possible remedy would be to improve the fine adjustment mechanism.

During the march from Tobruk to the battlefront, two out of 11 PzSfl 2 failed. The main cause was the engine which is generally considered to lack sufficient power. Subsequently a maximum speed of 10kph was ordered, but this makes the Sfl much slower than a tank, and this is tactically unacceptable. The rear leaf springs on the running gear are too fragile, and the centre bolts break

Five PzSfl 2 of the 12 delivered to North Africa assembled in an oasis to re-arm and refuel. The PzKpfw 38(t) chassis proved to be very reliable when operating over, sometimes rocky, desert terrain.

frequently. The bolts on track links are some 15mm too long and these break off easily due to the rocky terrain. After a short time of running the engine exhaust begins to glow red and could be a fire hazard. The internal main stowage for ammunition is unmanageable and takes too long to load. This main stowage should be used as a reserve, with ready-to-fire rounds stowed in armoured boxes mounted on the exterior.

Far left: The 7.5cm PaK 40 was the most powerful anti-tank gun deployed by German forces in North Africa.

Résumè

By end of 1942, the German tank destroyer units in North Africa had been issued with effective weapons. The 5cm PaK 38 proved to be an excellent gun and the outstanding performance of the 7.62cm PaK 36 made it capable of defeating any British armour at long range, including the newly-arrived US-supplied M4 Sherman and the British-built Infantry Tank Mk IV Churchill. With the gun mounted on a half-track chassis, the *Panzerjäger* were able to follow an attack and provide precious supporting fire. An unknown number of the comparable 7.5cm PaK 40, were issued in 1943 only.

In November 1942, Rommel was forced to send an urgent message to *Generalfeldmarschall* Keitel, which caused much alarm. Rommel stated that battle losses suffered by Axis (Italian-German) forces were not being replenished and that sufficient vital supplies were not being delivered. Subsequently he was faced with a disaster.

Panzerarmee Afrika – target/actual comparison November 1942										
	Panzer		**PzSpWg**		**PaK**		**8.8cm FlaK**		**2cm FlaK**	
	actual	target	actual	target	actual	target	actual	target	actual	target
DAK (15. and 21.PzDiv)	35	371	16	60	12	246	0	0	0	0
90.le Div	0	71	4	30	31	229	0	0	0	0
164.le Div	0	0	0	4	2	208	0	0	0	0
PzGrenRgt Afrika	0	0	0	0	14	54	0	0	0	0
19.FlaDiv	0	0	0	0	0	0	40	72	60	225
Brigade Ramcke	0	0	0	0	21	102	0	0	0	0

The overstretched German war machine had been unable to provide sufficient men, tanks, artillery and other weapons, to win the battle for North Africa.

Rommel was recalled to Germany on 9 March 1943, and *Panzerarmee Afrika* surrendered on 13 May 1943.

The year 1942 was earmarked as being decisive for German strategic targets. After the humiliating defeat at Moscow, Hitler as the new self-proclaimed *Oberkommandierender der Wehrmacht* (supreme army commander), decided to stop further offensive operations of *Heeresgruppe Mitte*, now prioritizing the rich oil fields of Baku and Maikop. Russia's southern areas with their oil field in the Caucasus should become target of a new large offensive called *Unternehmen* Blau (Blue). As with the attack on the Soviet Union one year before, for meteorological reasons the month of June was chosen.

In accordance with Hitler the OrgAbt was keen to deliver as much modern equipment as possible. The term *Langrohr* (abbreviated to *lang*) for long-barreled guns became symptomatic. Beside the improved versions of the PzKpfw III with 5cm KwK L/60 and PzKpfw IV with 7.5cm KwK L/43, introduction of effective anti-tank guns was promoted as the first result of the s PaK programme.

At approximately the same time in the early summer of 1942 production of the s PaK, new effective anti-tank guns, started.

Production and delivery would, however, take time. The troops were forced to work with what they had, often insufficient material.

On 4 May 1942, *Heeresgruppe Mitte* informed its attached units about methods of destroying enemy tanks that could not be defeated with the existing anti-tank weapons:

> The army group gives notice of experiences in destroying enemy tanks by a company of 251.InfDiv (IX.*Armee*):

When sufficient 7.5cm PaK 40 became available military planners decided to order an improved vehicle utilizing the PzKpfw 38(t) chassis, since it had proven to be a rugged and reliable platform. The vehicle was to be fitted with a superstructure which significantly improved protection for the crew. All variants using this chassis were known as *Marder* ([pine] marten) III.

The Renault UE *Beute-Schlepper* (captured tractor), here towing a 5cm PaK 38, was generally popular with anti-tank gun crews since it had good off-road mobility. But the type lacked space, requiring the gun crew and ammunition to be transported on another vehicle.

The division gave orders to blow up some tanks [three T-34] lying behind the *Hauptkampflinie* [HKL – main line of resistance] with explosives. We took this opportunity to perform trial blasts.

The T-Mine proved to be the most effective weapon when placed on the turret. In three cases the tank burned out totally.

Three 3kg explosive devices jammed into the gun barrel blew it to pieces.

On 25 March, an immobilized T-34 laying 200m behind the our HKL was destroyed during darkness by *Stosstruppen* (combat squads) using explosive charges. Three 1kg *Sprengbüchse* (explosive charge) were placed in the gun barrel and a 5kg explosive charge on the turret. The tank burnt out.

On 30 March several enemy tanks broke through our front-line positions. Of the four KV-1 heavy tanks which attacked the village, three remained on the outskirts and one crossed the area. This was effectively halted by a T-Mine thrown in front of the tracks; another was placed on the engine deck destroying the cover plate. A hand grenade thrown down the gun barrel had no visible impact and a *geballte Ladung* (amalgamated charge) of seven hand grenades which was thrown onto the turret roof had no effect either, the turret still rotated and the crew was not affected. However, two T-Mines placed under the turret overhang exploded and ripped it off its mounting ring, killing two crewmen. The remaining crew was silenced with hand grenades.

During the afternoon a second KV-1 was attacked with two T-Mines and halted, the ammunition exploding as it burnt out.

It is definitely feasible for a combat team to immobilize and destroy an enemy tank, but it will always require much courage and boldness from a commander and his men.

However, in the mentioned events single tanks without cover of accompanying infantry were attacked. Close combat against tanks was perilous.

In January 1942, *SS-Polizei-Division* (SS-PolDiv – police division), basically organized as an infantry division, was attached to *Heeresgruppe Nord* (Army Group North) deployed against the Volkhov Front – a major formation of the Red Army commanded by General Meretskov. A KStN, published at the time, shows that the unit was supposed to be equipped with 75 of the reliable 3.7cm PaK anti-tank guns, 36 of the versatile 10.5cm leFH 18 and also four 8.8cm FlaK.

On 18 May 1942, SS-PolDiv submitted a report of their experiences attacking Russian tanks:

Effect of the *Stielgranate* [stick grenade] on most types of enemy tanks, including the KV-1, was usually effective at a range of up to 100m. But were ineffective against a T-34.

Example: 14./PolSchtzRgt 2 fired stick grenades at several T-34 tanks. Some 19 direct hits were observed, but without success.

Commitment of 3.7cm PaK firing PzGr 38 or PzGr 40 (tungsten core) ammunition was only partially successful.

Example: By firing accurately at the rear-drive sprocket wheel or the turret-mounting ring a T-34 was temporarily put out of action – turret jammed, mobility severely impaired. Any Soviet light tank hit by a PzGr 40 was destroyed.

Since no 5cm PaK or Russian-built 7.62cm PaK anti-tank guns were available, no experiences can be reported.

A Soviet tank commander, especially of a T-34, will choose not use rough tracks or gaps through woodland but would always seek open terrain. In dense woodland the 3.7cm PaK was always inferior despite many trees being felled to give open lines of fire. The mines we laid were either cleared by enemy engineers, or were detonated by MG fire from a tank. Despite this experience, anti-tank mine belts are still the most important weapon against an enemy tank, but a single belt is not sufficient; every time two belts were used a T-34 was immobilized.

In the dense forest, a 10.5cm le FH 18 could defeat an enemy tank, but only at a range of around 200m. To be effective the gun must be deployed in groups of two or three; a single gun will be attacked and inevitably destroyed. The *Rotkopf-Munition* [red top ammunition] fired from the weapon simply ricocheted off the armour of both the KV-1 and T-34.

There has been no instance reported where a close-combat team has been successful at destroying a moving tank. However, any enemy tank immobilized on the battlefield was successfully attacked with *Hohlladung* [shaped charge], satchel charges and flamethrowers.

The few PzKpfw III tanks attached to the division were successful in destroying three light tanks and three armoured cars.

Enemy tanks destroyed during the fighting from 15 March to 5 May 1942:

Five KV-1 tanks by 3.7cm PaK firing *Stielgranate*
Three T-34 tanks by 3.7cm PaK firing *Stielgranate*
Three T-34 by 10.5cm le FH 18 firing *Rotkopf*.
One T-34 by 3.7cm PaK firing PzGr 40, a lucky shot which detonated fuel cans on the rear deck.
One light tank by 5cm PaK firing PzGr 40.
The number of T-34 tanks destroyed by close-combat teams was 21

In June 1942, the SS-PolDiv reported that it had lost almost all of its anti-tank weapons, which included the 5cm PaK 38 or 7.62cm FK 296(r), and had been informed not to expect any replacements in the near future. Although not a typical infantry division, this would decisively affect the combat value of the unit, but it continued to fight by using any available weapon including the 3.7cm PaK firing a *Stielgranate* (stick grenade with shaped charge). A field howitzer could be used but only at short range. The most likely outcome of a determined attack by enemy tanks supported by infantry would be possible annihilation.

On 27 March 1942, AOK 2 submitted an appraisal of German anti-tank defence to the *Heeresgruppe Süd* (Army Group South):

1) All previously issued anti-tank weapons are regarded as lacking the performance required to effectively defeat the latest Soviet tanks encountered on the battlefront. During the winter it was necessary to call for support from artillery and 8.8cm FlaK units.

2) However, the *Panzerjäger* have an immediate requirement for more powerful guns. At the moment the tank destroyer companies have a wide range of weapon types, and can be supported by 8.8cm FlaK, *Sturmgeschütz* and the artillery.
But this number of different guns leads, inevitably, to problems: training, equipment and ammunition supply and battlefield organization. One

example is the order to reinforce anti-tank defences (OKH/OrgAbt [III] Nr.1155/42 dated 9 March 1942), which led to the allotment of three different types of anti-tank gun for a PzJgKp.

3) The enemy deploys tanks to effectively overcome the defensive fire, especially machine gun, of our infantry and then continue to advance and destroy our artillery. The most effective weapon against an enemy tank is the *Panzerabwehrkanone*, either towed or *Selbstsfahrlafette* [self-propelled]: also, the 8.8cm FlaK is proving to be an effective weapon. Currently there are a number of heavier anti-tank weapons in production, including self-propelled, and deliveries will begin soon.

4) We wish to reiterate that we already have a most effective weapon available – the *Sturmgeschütz*. On numerous occasions the type remained in action after all other artillery weapons had failed – anti-tank guns due to their ineffective calibre also the light field howitzers and FlaK guns which were difficult to manoeuvre.

5) We now question if it is possible to modify the *Sturmgeschütz*:
   – Is an increase in calibre from 7.5cm to 8.8cm possible?
   – Should the original gun mounting be retained or a tank-type rotating turret be fitted?

The *Rauppenschlepper-OST* was specifically developed to operate, in all weathers, on the poor roads and tracks encountered during the advance into the Soviet Union. For reliability, the vehicle was fitted with a very noisy air-cooled diesel engine; any usage near the frontline was extremely hazardous. The vehicle is towing a 5cm PaK 38 mounted on snow skids.

A PzSfl 2 mounting a 7.62cm PaK 36(r) on the battlefront in early summer 1942. Note the German censor has obliterated the muzzle brake. (SZ Photo)

6) We suggest issuing each division with a *Sturmgeschütz-Abteilung*, thus allowing each to have not only an infantry support gun, but also an effective anti-tank weapon.

7) The side armour on the hull of a *Sturmgeschütz* is known to be vulnerable and will be targeted by the enemy. To prevent this the vehicle must be protected by supporting fire from mobile 2cm FlaK units. Urgent consideration should be given to strengthening each of the standard three StuG batteries to have two 2cm FlaK batteries attached. This would not only provide more support fire, but also fill an urgent requirement for better anti-aircraft defences.

8) In conclusion we suggest the following structure:
   – An infantry *Panzerjäger-Kompanie* in the previous form but equipped with 7.5cm PaK.
   – A *Sturmgeschütz-Abteilung* with three StuG batteries and two batteries of self-propelled 2cm FlaK.

9) Ultimately the *Panzerjäger* and *Sturmartillerie* [assault artillery] could be combined.

This appraisal identifies the problems affecting many German army units, particularly infantry divisions, in the early months of 1942. The document concludes by identifying the requirement for self-propelled guns and the use of *Sturmgeschütz* for anti-tank warfare. However, this was not exactly new; after *Unternehmen* Barbarossa the majority of infantry divisions had requested an integral assault gun unit. Also, the requirement for more powerful ordnance to make the *Sturmgeschütz* a more versatile support weapon had been lodged in 1939. At that time the 8.8cm FlaK was also being used for fighting armour and pillboxes.

The shortage of material and production capacity in Germany made it impossible for any ambitious plans to be made in 1940, or even by the end of 1942. Large-scale deliveries of *Sturmgeschütz* to infantry units finally began in mid-1943, but only in sufficient numbers to equip a company and not a battalion.

Special Purpose Weapons

Hitler was an enthusiast of heavily armed and armoured weapons which would be deployed against well-defended enemy positions. In 1941, the PzSfl IVa self-propelled gun, armed with a modified 10cm *Kanone* 18 as a *Schartenbrecher* (bunker buster), entered service but only two were ever built.

In 1942 the PzSfl V, built on a modified Henschel VK 30.01(H) chassis (prototype for the Tiger) mounting a Rheinmetall-built 12.8cm K40 L/60 gun, entered service. Two were completed and delivered to PzJgAbt 521 (*Heeresgruppe Süd*) where they were deployed on the Eastern Front, with the sole surviving PzSfl IVa, as heavy tank destroyers.

However, due to only two being built, their effect in combat has to be evaluated as negligible, but all experience gained did influence the development of later self-propelled types.

Introduction and Distribution of s PaK

In April 1943 the high command of 2.*Panzerarmee* published details of their new plan to reorganize the tank destroyer elements in infantry divisions. This entailed the allocation of the different types of heavy anti-tank gun which had been available since mid-1942. Due to material, production and technical problems when production of the s PaK began, it had been impossible to concentrate all efforts on one universal type. Instead a number of different guns were produced for the military.

Due to the lack of suitable towing vehicles, many tank destroyer units were provisionally equipped with agricultural tractors. Two 7.62cm PaK 36(r) anti-tank guns, from PzJgAbt 251 (251. InfDiv), are being towed by Hanomag K50 crawler tractors. Attached to each gun is a box-type sledge carrying ammunition and supplies.

Since the tank destroyer elements of the three *Grenadierregimenter* (rifle regiments) were concentrated in the 14.Kp each were to be supplied with either:

Two heavy PaK (7.5cm PaK 97/38)
Two medium PaK (5cm PaK 38 or 4.5cm PaK[r])
Six light PaK (3.7cm PaK)
Six MG 34

or

Four medium Pak (5cm PaK 38 or 4.5cm PaK[r])
Six light PaK (3.7cm PaK)
Six MG 34

OKH/GenStbdH
Performance overview of all armour-piercing weapons and ammunition 15 September 1942
Infantry weapons, light and medium anti-tank guns
Shaped-charge round show identical penetration data at all combat ranges

Weapon	Ammunition	Type	Penetration	Comment in file	Author's remark
Rifle	GePzGr 30	Shaped-charge	50mm		
	Gr GePzGr	Shaped-charge	70–80mm		
PzB 39	Gr GePzGr	Shaped-charge	70–80mm		
2cm FlaK	2cm StielGr	Shaped-charge	120mm	Under development	Never introduced
2.5cm PaK 112(f)	2.5cm StielGr	Shaped-charge	140mm	Under development	Never introduced
2.8cm sPB 41	2.8cm PzGrPatr 41	Tungsten V° 1,430mps	60mm at 100m Carbide (HVAP)	40mm at 500m 24mm at 1,000m	
3.7cm PaK	3.7cm StielGr 41	Shaped-charge	180mm		
4.2cm PaK 41	4.2cm PzGrPatr	Tungsten 41 V° 1,350mps	100mm at 100m Carbide (HVAP)	60mm at 500m 25mm at 1,000m	
4.7cm PaK(t)	4.7cm StielGr(t)	Shaped-charge	180mm	Under development	Never introduced
4.7cm PaK 181(f)	4.7cm StielGr(f)	Shaped-charge	180mm	Under development	Never introduced
5cm PaK 38 5cm KwK 39 (L/60)	5cm PzGrPatr 39 V° 835mps	Composite (APCBC)	65mm at 100m 60mm at 500m	51mm at 1,000m	
	5cm PzGrPatr 40 V° 1,200mps	Tungsten Carbide (HVAP)	120mm at 100m 75mm at 500m	40mm at 1,000m	

OKH/GenStbdH
Performance overview of all armour-piercing weapons and ammunition 15 September 1942
7.5cm – weapons, s PaK
Shaped-sharge round show identical penetration data at all combat ranges

Weapon	Ammunition	Type	Penetration	Comment in file	Author's remark
7.5cm KwK 40 (L/48) 7.5cm StuK 40 (L/48)	7.5cm PzGrPatr 39 V° 770mps	Composite (APCBC)	105mm at 100m 95mm at 500m 80mm at 1,000m		
	7.5cm PzGrPatr 40 V° 990mps	Tungsten Carbide (HVAP)	145mm at 100m 125mm at 500m 100mm at 1,000m		
	7.5cm Gr 38 (HL/A)	Shaped charge	70mm		
	7.5cm Gr 38 (HL/B)	Shaped-charge	75mm		
7.5cm PaK 40 (L/46) motorized traction and Sfl	7.5cm PzGrPatr 39 V° 770mps	Composite (APCBC)	100mm at 100m 90mm at 500m 80mm at 1,000m		
	7.5cm PzGrPatr 40 V° 990 m/s	Tungsten Carbide (HVAP)	140mm at 100m 125mm at 500m 100mm at 1,000m		
	7.5cm Gr 38 (HL/A)	Shaped-charge	70mm		
	7.5cm Gr 38 (HL/B)	Shaped-charge	75mm		
7.5cm PaK 41	7.5cm PzGrPatr 41	APCNR Tungsten carbide or steel	190mm at 100m 165mm at 500m 130mm at 1,000m		
7.5cm PaK 36 (r) motorized traction and Sfl	7.62 cm PzGrPatr 39 V° 740mps	Composite (APCBC)	96mm at 100m 90mm at 500m 80mm at 1,000m		
	7.62cm PzGrPatr 40 V° 990mps	Tungsten Carbide (HVAP)	145mm at 100m 125mm at 500m 100mm at 1,000m		
	7.5cm Gr 38 (HL/A)	Shaped-charge	70mm		
	7.5cm Gr 38 (HL/B)	Shaped-charge	75mm		
5cm PaK 38 5cm KwK 39 (L/60)	5cm PzGrPatr 39 V° 835mps	Composite (APCBC)	65mm at 100m 60mm at 500m 51mm at 1,000m		
	5cm PzGrPatr 40 V° 1,200mps	Tungsten Carbide (HVAP)	120 mm at 100m 75mm at 500m 40mm at 1,000m		
7.5cm PaK 97/38	7.5cm Gr 38 (HL/A)	Shaped-charge	70mm		
	7.5cm Gr 38 (HL/B)	Shaped-charge	75mm		

OKH/GenStbdH
Performance overview of all armour-piercing weapons and ammunition 15 September 1942
Artillery
Shaped-charge round show identical penetration data to all combat ranges

Weapon	Ammunition	Type	Penetration	Comment in file	Author's remark
7.5cm LG 1 7.5cm le FK 18	7.5cm Gr 38 (HL/A)	Shaped-charge	70mm		
7.5cm le IG 18 7.5cm Geb IG 18 7.5cm Feb G 36 7.5cm Geb K 15	7.5cm Gr 38 (HL/B)	Shaped-charge	75mm		
10cm LG 40 (Kp) 10cm LG 42 (Rh)	10cm Gr HL/A 10cm Gr 39 HL/B	Shaped-charge Shaped-charge	80mm 90mm		
10.5cm le FH 16 10.5cm le FH 18	10cm Gr 39 rot HL/A	Shaped-charge	80mm		
10.5cm Geb H 40 10cm K 131 (f)	10cm Gr 39 rot HL/b	Shaped-charge	90mm		
12.8cm K 40	12.8cm PzGrPatr	Composite	150mm at 1,000m		
15cm sIG 33	15cm Gr 39 HL/A	Shaped-charge	130mm	Under development	Introduced in 1943
15cm sFH 18 15cm sFH 36 15cm sFH 42	15cm Gr 39 HL/A	Shaped-charge	130mm	Under development	Introduced in 1943
15.5cm sFH 414 (f)	15.5cm Gr 39 HL/A (f)	Shaped-charge	140mm	Under development	Introduction questionable
7.5cm LG 40	7.5cm Gr 38 (HL/B)	Shaped-charge	75mm		
10.5cm K 331(f)	10cm Gr 39 HL/B (f)	Shaped-charge	90mm		

OKH/GenStbdH
Performance overview of all armour-piercing weapons and ammunition 15 September 1942
Close-combat weapons

Weapon	Ammunition	Type	Penetration	Comment in file	Author's remark
Blendkörper BK 1H	Dazzling grenade	Oval glass container	Dazzling effect. Irritant effect when entering the interior		
T-Mine 35	5kg explosives	Explosive	80–100mm		
Geballte Ladung	3kg explosives	Concentrated explosive charges	60mm		Penetration data given is questionable
Hafthohlladung 3kg	1.5kg explosives	Shaped-charge	140mm	Splinter and pressure effect in the interior	

OKH/GenStbdH
Performance overview of all armour-piercing weapons and ammunition 15 September 1942

Weapon	Ammunition	Type	Penetration	Comment in file	Author's remark
Rifle	GePzGr 30	Hollow charge	50mm		
	Gr GePzGr	Hollow charge	70–80mm		
PzB 39	Gr GePzGr	Hollow charge	70–80mm		
2cm FlaK	2cm Stielgranate	Hollow charge	120mm	Under development	Never introduced
2.5cm Pak 112(f)	2.5cm Stielgranate	Hollow charge	140mm	Under devlopment	Never introduced
2.8cm sPB 41	2.8cm PzGrPatr 41 V° 1,430mps	Tungsten Carbide			

The divisional *Panzerjäger-Abteilung* was to receive three companies, each having:

Six heavy PaK (7.62cm PaK 36 or 7.5cm PaK 41 or 7.5cm PaK 97/38)
Four light PaK (3.7cm PaK)
Six MG 34

The above indicates that there were not sufficient numbers of s PaK available to complete an equal reorganization of the PzJgKp. For reasons of mobility, tank destroyer elements (14.Kp) positioned with the front-line infantry were equipped with French-built 7.5cm PaK 97/38, which was some 235kg lighter than a 7.5cm PaK 40.

The divisional tank destroyer battalion received a larger allocation of more effective s PaK; primarily the 7.62cm PaK 36 (re-bored breech), or 7.5cm PaK 41. If either of these was unavailable, the battalion would be supplied with the less effective 7.5cm PaK 97/38.

The *Rüststand* tables generated by the *Waffenamt* details production figures and numbers available at the front. But they are incomplete, since they have not clearly differentiated between the types available; the tables only show amalgamated figures for the 7.5cm PaK 40 (including Marder I, II and III) also 7.62cm PaK 36(r), combined with PzSfl 1 and 2.

Towed Anti-tank Weapons

After realizing that the 76.2mm field gun M1936 used by the Red Army – large numbers had been captured intact – had an impressive anti-tank performance, German infantry and *Panzerjäger* units became eager to acquire as many of the type as possible. Those guns that were not

Development of stocks of German anti-tank guns.

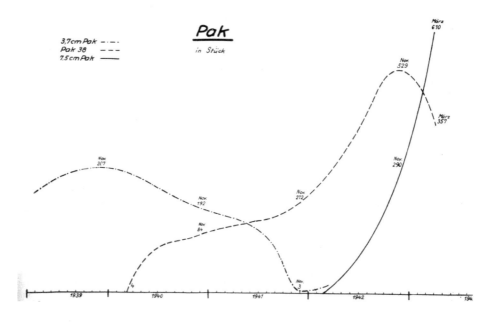

Development of anti-tank and tank gun ammunition (x1,000).

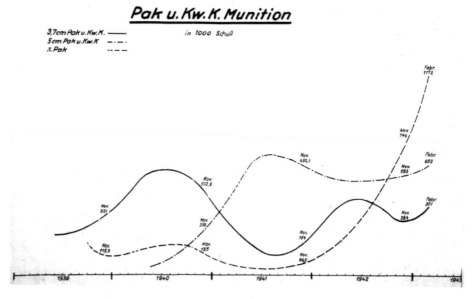

immediately utilized by advancing units were transported to storage areas and allocated to front-line units as required.

Designated 7.62cm *Feldkanone* (*russisch*) (FK[r] – field gun [Russian]) the gun did not require any modification since a commensurate amount of Soviet ammunition had also been captured. In September 1941, the OrgAbt decided to send a substantial number of surplus guns to the *Afrika Korps* in North Africa.

In 1942, the first of four types resulting from the s PaK programme began to be delivered in slowly increasing numbers to front-line units. However, in April 1942 and following a *Führerweisung* (Führer command), the OrgAbt announced that production of towed and self-propelled anti-tank guns was to be accelerated so that by May sufficient numbers would be available for *Fall Blau* (Case Blue), the Caucasus offensive planned for 28 June 1942:

- 150: 7.5cm PaK 40
- 150: 7.5cm PaK 41
- 150: 7.62cm PaK 36(r) (mot Z)
- 120: 7.62cm PaK 36(r) on Sfl CKD [PzKpfw 38(t)]
- 130: 7.62cm PaK 36(r) on Sfl PzKpfw II
- 800: 7.5cm PaK 97/38(f)

A report published by the OrgAbt in September 1942 notes that most of the requirements were realized or exceeded:

- *Heeresgruppe Süd* received 360 7.5cm PaK 40 and 425 7.5cm PaK 97/38.

A 7.5cm PaK 41, high-velocity anti-tank gun, attached to an SdKfz 10. This reliable and low-profile vehicle was regarded, by those on the frontline, as the best light half-track tractor in service.

- *Heeresgruppe Mitte* received 141 7.5cm PaK 41, 150 7.62cm PaK 36(r) and 295 7.5cm PaK 97/38.
- *Heeresgruppe Nord* received 150 7.62cm PaK 36(r) and 150 7.5cm PaK 97/38.

Far left: The PzSfl 2, like most self-propelled guns, offered no protection to the crew against the weather. The usage of the travelling cradle was mandatory, since frequent movement of the gun (7.62cm PaK 36[r]) barrel often caused damage to the gun mounting.

Self-propelled s PaK

At the same time as the s PaK anti-tank gun was being supplied to front-line units, a number of self-propelled s Pak were being delivered to selected units.

The PzSfl 1, built on the chassis of a PzKpfw II, was supplied to infantry divisions (including some SS units) and also to four independent Heeres-*Panzerjäger-Abteilungen* (HPzJgAbt – army tank destroyer battalions).

The PzSfl 2, built on the chassis of a PzKpfw 38(t), was issued to tank divisions, also an independent HPzJgAbt and to those units transferred to *Panzerarmee Afrika*.

Documents of the time, indicate that the numbers involved varied widely; somewhere between six and 20 were issued.

It is interesting to note that KStN 1148a, dated 15 February 1942, also includes the allotment of ammunition carriers. The type utilized the chassis of an obsolete PzKpfw I fitted with a box-like superstructure and were delivered with an SdAnh 31 trailer. There is documentary evidence that units equipped with PzSfl 2 were also issued PzKpfw 38(t) as *Panzerbefehlswagen* (armoured command vehicles).

Although the SdKfz 10 was very popular with anti-tank gun crews, being quiet to operate and easy to conceal from enemy observers, but like other German half-track types it was costly and complicated to produce: This resuted in a constant shortage for front-line units.

The tank destroyer units were often provided with obsolete PzKpfw I or II which had been modified as ammunition carriers. Here a PzKpfw II has been fitted with an armoured superstructure and the *Maschinengewehr* (MG – machine gun) ball mounting taken from a damaged PzKpfw III.

Special Purpose Weapons

In late 1941, the first of a number of decisions were made to effectively reinforce the *Panzerjägertruppe* with heavy anti-tank weapons and the KStNs adjusted accordingly.

A new combined *Kriegsgliederung* (order of battle), published in September 1942, detailed the very different ways that the latest equipment would be issued.

In September 1942, the combat state of the Panzer divisions caused considerable concern. Most were in a significantly weakened state as stated in this hand-written note attached to a *Kriegsgliederung*; 'reduced mobility, not refurbished'. The most badly affected were 1.PzDiv, 2.PzDiv, 3.PzDiv, 5.PzDiv, 8.PzDiv, 12.PzDiv, 17.PzDiv, 18.PzDiv, 19.PzDiv and 20.PzDiv since each had only one operational tank battalion.

All other divisions reported that they had the standard allotment of two tank battalions, but they did not indicate the exact number of combat-ready tanks. To complicate matters further: In mid-1942 deliveries of the PzKpfw IV began, firstly in small numbers but this steadily increased.

In contrast, the *Panzerjäger* units were increased drastically, possibly as a result of the defeat at Moscow where German forces had been overwhelmed by Soviet armour.

The *Kriegsgliederungen* dated September 1942, shows that there were many variations as to how units were formed and equipped. In principle, a divisional PzJgAbt was formed as follows: towed anti-tank gun, self-propelled gun and anti-aircraft elements. But a generalization is impossible since the exact composition could vary depending on the availability of personnel, equipment and weaponry or if a unit was in the process of being re-formed and re-equipped. Also, a number of units could have been reinforced in the field.

Panzer Division

The allotment of anti-tank weapons within a Panzer division varied widely, which makes it almost impossible to generalize. The only common factor was four *Schützen-Battailone* (rifle battalions) each having a *schwere Kompanie* (s Kp – heavy companies) which had a *Panzerjäger-Zug* (PzJgZug – anti-tank platoon) equipped with three s PaK. The *Aufklärungs-Abteilung* (AufkAbt – reconnaissance battalion) also had a heavy company available.

A damaged PzSfl 2, on a SdAnh 115, ready to be transported by rail to a repair depot. An ever-present lack of replacement vehicles forced German units to recover any that were battle damaged or had failed mechanically.

The composition of a divisional PzJgAbt could also be very different; PzJgAbt 38 (2.PzDiv) had two towed anti-tank gun companies, a self-propelled tank destroyer battalion and a self-propelled FlaK company: PzJgAbt 543 (3.PzDiv) was issued with two towed anti-tank gun companies and a self-propelled FlaK company, whereas PzJgAbt 92 (20.PzDiv) had a towed anti-tank gun company, two self-propelled tank destroyer companies and a self-propelled FlaK company.

Waffen-SS Units

Following demands made by high-ranking officials of the *Waffen-SS*, the anti-tank elements in the divisions Liebstandarte-Adolf Hitler, Das Reich, Totenkopf, and Wiking were significantly improved and were equipped to a similar standard as that of an army Panzer division.

A PzSfl 2 in service with a training and replacement unit. To save anti-tank ammunition an MG 34 has been mounted on the gun barrel which, by firing tracer bullets, allowed the gunner to be trained on how to sight the gun.

Infantry Division (mot)

Motorized infantry divisions such as 3.InfDiv (mot) had towed anti-tank weapons at regimental level. Each of the two staff companies were issued with three s PaK and their six infantry battalions each had three m PaK (5cm PaK 38). The divisional tank destroyer battalion of 3. InfDiv (mot) (PzJgAbt 3) had two PzJgKp (Sfl), equipped with six PzSfl 1, and a towed PzJgKp with nine s PaK. The *Kradschützen* battalion had a smaller anti-tank gun detachment equipped with of three s PaK. In contrast, the infantry regiments in 10.InfDiv (mot) had 24 towed anti-tank guns, but the PzJgAbt had only three towed anti-tank gun companies. The anti-tank gun detachment in the *Kradschützen* (motorcycle infantry) battalion was equipped with three s PaK.

Other, but not all InfDivs (mot) had also a FlaKp (Sfl) equipped with 12 SdKfz 10/4 [2cm FlaK 30] or 10/5 [2cm FlaK 38] self-propelled anti-aircraft guns.

The PzSfl 2 offered only small amount of space for the crew to stow personal equipment and supplies. Here the crew has placed six cans, containing petrol, on the superstructure. The gun is supported, a mandatory requirement for the 7.62cm PaK 36(r), in the travelling cradle.

Deliveries of replacement vehicles were never consistent and this led to many tank destroyer units operating a variety of types. The nearest vehicle is a Marder III, and the other a PzSfl 2. Although both used the PzKpfw 38(t) chassis and fired the same ammunition, the 7.62cm PaK 36(r) and the 7.5cm PaK 40 were completely different weapons which increased the number of spare parts to be carried.

InfDiv Grossdeutschland (GD)

As an elite crack unit, each of the infantry regiments in GD was issued with a PzJgKp (Sfl) equipped with six PzSfl 1. The divisional PzJgAbt was issued with a PzJgKp (Sfl) equipped with six PzSfl 1 and also two PzJgKp equipped with nine towed s PaK. The unit was supported by a StuGAbt equipped with 21 StuG *lang* (long).

Infantry Division

In September 1939, a standard infantry division was normally issued with only towed anti-tank weapons. However, in 1942 the situation changed and the three infantry regiments in a division were issued with three *teilbewegliche* (semi-mobile) anti-tank companies with vehicle-towed guns and horse-drawn supply elements. These companies could be issued with the 5cm PaK 38 or the 7.5cm PaK 97/38, the 7.62cm PaK 38 or the 7.5cm PaK in a variety of combinations. The heavy company in a reconnaissance battalion had a platoon equipped with three 5cm PaK 38. The divisional PzJgAbt was intended to be fully mobile and was issued with three companies equipped with three s PaK and eight m PaK.

The reasoning behind exactly how and why anti-tank weapons were allocated remains unknown and the published strength tables must be regarded as a planning target. In reality there were many variations due mainly to the many problems faced by the German armaments industry. The allotment of equipment was always subject to availability; it was not uncommon for front-line units to be issued with three or even four different types of anti-tank gun. If there were no heavy anti-tank guns available, units would have to accept smaller calibre guns, but rarely the number requested. Mounting losses on the battlefront also aggravated the situation.

As an example PzJgAbt 37 (1.PzDiv) was reorganized in July 1942 and reported the following strength in September: The 1.Kp had been issued with six PzJg 38(t) 7.62cm PaK 36 (PzSfl 2). Both 2.Kp and 3.Kp were each to be issued with six s PaK and four m PaK. The 4.Kp provided anti-aircraft defence.

However, records show that 3./PzJgAbt 37 could not be established as planned.

On 25 November 1942, after being transferred to near Kolm [Cholm], PzJgAbt 37 submitted a more accurate strength report:

An NCO of 23.PzDiv checks the condition of the muzzle brake on the 7.5cm PaK 40/2 of a Marder II.

The first Marder II were built on the chassis of a PzKpfw II Ausf A or Ausf C and armed with the 7.6cm PaK 36(r). A second version utilized a PzKpfw II Ausf F chassis and mounted a 7.5cm PaK 40 L/46 in a lower and more spacious superstructure. Both proved to be mechanically reliable and effective in combat.

2.) After transfer the following weapons and vehicles are operational:

2.Kp: No artillery tractors available.

Guns: One 7.5cm PaK 41
        Four 7.5cm PaK 97/38
        One 7.62cm PaK 36
Tractors: Two ZgKw (starter motors damaged)
        Two Opel 3t Typ A trucks
Losses: One 7.5cm PaK 41, transferred to workshop in Ivaniki
        Two ZgKw (engine, gearbox and suspension damaged)
        Two Ford trucks (engine and electrical system damaged)

3.Kp:

Guns: Four Sfl
        Three Munitions-Schlepper
Losses: One Sfl
        One PzKpfw 38(t)
        Two PzKpfw 38(t) without superstructure

Despite the German doctrine of highly mobile warfare, many units were never adequately equipped with half-track vehicles or trucks suitable for towing artillery guns. Here the crew of a 7.5cm PaK 97/38 anti-tank gun has attached the weapon to a limber hauled by a team of four-horses.

3.Kp has only one Opel 3-ton truck to use as a rations and supply vehicle. The 4.Kp (FlaK) will report later.

This strength report needs clarification: what remained of 1.Kp and 2.Kp had been amalgamated, so subsequently there is no reference to 1.Kp. Three different types of heavy anti-tank gun are noted – 7.5cm PaK 41, 7.62cm PaK 36 and 7.5cm PaK 97/38 – and is somewhat incomprehensible. Each type fired three basic types of ammunition (each had several subtypes), a constant supply of which had to be delivered. Military planners in the Reich had again proved unable to supply sufficient [same calibre] weapons to enable front-line troops to fight effectively.

A 7.5cm PaK 97/38 in service with a Waffen-SS unit has been attached to an RSO fully-tracked tractor. Although the vehicle had outstanding off-road performance, it was very difficult to steer accurately.

The overall low numbers of available guns is evidence of the heavy losses due to hard fighting. Again a comparison of the authorized strength in 1.Kp and 2.Kp is interesting; in November 1942 only six out of 20 towed anti-tank guns were available, while 3.Kp had three of its six PzSfl 2 still operational.

Surprisingly, PzJgAbt 37 seems to have had a relatively large number of *Munitionswagen* (ammunition carriers) in service, but the reason for this is unknown since no organizational structures have survived. The only relevant table, KStN 1148a, published on 15 February 1942. The majority of ammunition carriers were built on the chassis of redundant tanks and fitted with a box-shaped superstructure fabricated by engineers in field workshops. It is known that PzJgAbt 37 had at least five converted PzKpfw 38(t) including one for the company commander and another used as a radio vehicle.

The supply of suitable gun tractors was totally insufficient; the required numbers of the SdKfz 10 and SdKfz 11 half-track tractors were not being delivered, nor were there any suitable heavy cross-country cars or medium cargo trucks. In an attempt to solve the problem units began to receive agricultural tractors, but numbers delivered were dependent on availability.

3.7cm PaK

The 3.7cm PaK is often referred to as an ineffective weapon, and this is based on after-action reports which showed the gun as lacking firepower against heavily-armoured Soviet tanks even at close range. In summer 1940, military planners ordered that front-line forces were to receive a more powerful anti-tank gun; the 5cm PaK 38 (L/60) manufactured by Rheinmetall-Borsig. The gun would prove to be a reliable weapon but not totally effective for defeating a T-34 medium and more so the KV heavy tank.

However, while the *Panzerjäger* battalions continued to clamour for improved, heavier-calibre anti-tank guns. Whereas the tank destroyer platoons in infantry and rifle regiments remained content with the 3.7cm PaK, since it was the only towed anti-tank weapon which a crew could easily move around the battlefield. Many front-line units still regarded 3.7cm PaK as vital for providing effective fire support with high-explosive ammunition, or defeating enemy light tanks and armoured cars with armour-piercing rounds.

In January 1943, IX.*Armee* and *Heeresgruppe Mitte* were tasked with repelling Soviet counterattacks heading towards Smolensk. The command echelons submitted a combined after-action report:

> The 3.7cm PaK has proven very effective during the recent heavy attacks as well as during the fighting in August. Using various ammunition, we successfully fought against a wide variety of enemy tanks, T-60, T-70, US-built 'General Lee' and the T-34. The gun is very mobile, which was a great advantage. Even massed infantry attacks could be repelled. Firing HE shells, against point targets was possible, too. Since the battlefield is interrupted by small pieces of woodland, shallow recesses and bumps, the m PaK and s PaK cannot be used to full effect. To fill these gaps the light 3.7cm PaK is

irreplaceable. The *Stielgranate* (stick grenade) fired against massed infantry assaults had an incredible and devastating effect.

The 4.7cm PaK 181(f) [French-built 47mm APX] is not mobile enough due to its weight (1,070kg) and poor ground clearance. But since it is only effective at up to 400m range, it must be installed in front-line positions.

The 5cm PaK 38 shows clear penetration at ranges between 600m and 800m using the PzGr 39, even when a target is hit at an unfavourable angle. After the enemy tanks were destroyed, the gun could be effectively deployed to fire HE rounds on enemy infantry. Important, it is absolutely necessary for every enemy tank, even when immobilized, to be totally destroyed to preventing it being recovered.

A well-camouflaged 7.5cm PaK 40 in service with 5.SS-PzDiv Wiking positioned at the edge of a corn field.

Experience Reports

7.62cm PaK 36

In September 1942, despite urgent demands from front-line units, sufficient numbers of s PaK were not being manufactured, causing German military planners to examine the viability of using equipment captured from the Red Army. In 1942, the 76mm divisional gun M1936 was redesigned with a shorter gun barrel mounted on a lighter carriage. In Red Army service it was the 76mm ZiS 3, but captured guns were quickly re-designated as 7.62cm *Feldkanone*(r) (FK[r] – field gun [*russisch*-Russian]) 297. The OrgAbt reported:

> To make up for the shortage of s PaK, the Führer has ordered the immediate deployment of all available captured Russian 76mm [7.62cm] field guns although the performance of this weapon [with unchanged breech chamber] is some 10 to 15 per cent below that of the PaK 36(r).

For the anti-tank role, the Russian gun was bored out, to fire the slightly heavier German ammunition, and fitted with a muzzle brake to improve performance. The type was designated 7.62cm PaK 36(r).

A *Beuteschlepper* (captured tractor), possibly a Somua MCL-5, hauling a 7.62cm PaK 36(r) has become bogged down in deep mud. Many vehicles failed mechanically in such conditions.

In February 1943, *schnelle Abteilung* 290 (290.InfDiv) sent a favourable report on the Russian gun:

Combat experiences:

a) During the heavy defensive fighting from 15 and 19 February we achieved many successes using the s PaK 7.62cm(r):

b) All Russian tanks encountered (mainly T-34 and KV-1) were defeated by the 7.62cm PaK at ranges between 200m and 1,400m. One particular gun destroyed 11 tanks in less than an hour. Nine caught fire immediately and burnt out.

Advantages: The gun was very stable during firing, which made re-sighting easy. Rate of fire is sufficient due to it being semi-automatic. Accuracy is good when fired from a prepared position. Smaller deviations could be easily corrected thanks to tracer ammunition.

Disadvantages: The gun barrel is muzzle heavy and this makes the traversing mechanism stiff to operate; tracking a fast-moving tank is difficult. Due to the smoke from the muzzle brake being directed to the sides and takes too long to disperse, immediate re-sighting is impossible and often a target has moved.

In June 1943, PzJgAbt 36 conducted firing trials using a captured KV-1 (uparmoured) as the target and reported:

A 7.62cm PaK 36(r) almost perfectly camouflaged to blend in the winter landscape, The Soviet-built gun was an effective and versatile weapon which, although originally a field gun, proved to be a deadly anti-tank gun. In German service it was fitted with an improved gun shield, but this reduced elevation which affected usage as a field artillery gun.

The *Beutewaffen* (captured weapon) performed very well with different types of ammunition:

7.62cm PaK
    Range 100m, fire at turret and hull sides.
PzGrPatr 39
    Direct hit at hull armour, clear penetration.
    Range 300m, fire at turret and hull sides.
PzGrPatr 39
    Clear penetration a turret ring. After three hits the turret was lifted and shifted to the side for 40 – 50cm.
PzGrPatr 40
    Clear penetration at hull armour.
SprGrPatr 34
    Total destruction of running gear and tracks.
Conclusively it can be stated that the 7.62cm PaK 36 proved to be the most effective anti-tank weapon. Alternating fire with PzGrPatr 39 or PzGrPatr 40 and SprGrPatr 34 is recommended.

7.5cm PaK 40

In May 1942, 377.InfDiv received its first 7.5cm PaK 40. Some weeks later, on 19 June 1942 the unit submitted an after-action report:

Experience report on 7.5cm PaK 40:

Accuracy: No complaints
Penetration: At ranges from 500m to 600m at a 60-degree angle angle sufficient against T-34 and the British Infantry Tank Mk II (Matilda Mk IV).
Mobility: The gun is extremely rear heavy making it very difficult for the crew to move; it can only be pulled for 5m to 10m at a time.. The loss of one crew member would make this an impossible task; reserve personnel are essential. The *Unic-Schlepper* [U-304(f)] assigned as gun tractors are unsuitable, the vehicle is too high and conspicuous for front-line PzJg units.

Faults:
1) Rear heavy
2) Aiming and elevation mechanism are located too close together and difficult to operate, particularly if the crew are wearing gas masks.
3) The pneumatic equilibrators are fitted with simple cuff-type seals which frequently leak. Sudden shocks caused by rough terrain during the march,

and also the weight of the long barrel, will cause the oil to leak thus reduce pressure. We suggest the use of thicker oil and fitting better seals.

4) Tyres. The tread pattern is unsuitable: Stones and other foreign objects become stuck in the two grooves and will eventually rip the solid rubber to pieces.

In January 1943, an after-action report on the s PaK was delivered by 377. InfDiv to IX.*Armee*:

The 7.5cm PaK 40 (mot Z) has proved to be effective, but deployment is limited due to a lack of mobility and not having an armoured tractor. Also, the gun is too heavy for a crew to physically move. Therefore, it is most important to position the gun so that there is a clear line of fire at the selected target.

The 7.5cm PaK 40 (Sfl) is a very good weapon and our troops must learn to deploy it to utmost effect. The armour of the gun shield is too thin to protect the crew and this makes it important for the gun commander to seek a well-concealed firing position. Also, he must be encouraged to continuously search for new targets.

The above mentioned also applies to the deployment of the 7.62cm PaK.

Like the 5cm PaK 38, the carriage of a 7.5cm PaK 40 was carried on typical German-pattern steel wheels fitted with solid rubber tyres. Although these were bulletproof, stones could become jammed in the grooves and cause irreparable damage.

A 7.5cm PaK 40 positioned next to a farmhouse as the crew pose for the benefit of a propaganda photographer, but they have forgotten to remove the protective cover on the muzzle brake.

The French-built 7.5cm PaK 97/38(f), large numbers of which had been captured in 1940, remained in service with German forces until the end of the war. The gun had a performance similar to the 5cm PaK 38 when firing shaped-charge ammunition, but was more effective when using high-explosive rounds. Note, the gun is fitted with a muzzle brake.

7.5cm PaK 97/38

Beside 7.5cm PaK 40, the 377.InfDiv was issued with 7.5cm PaK 97/38:

> Accuracy: No complaints as with PaK 40
> Mobility: Despite the fact that the tail heaviness is weaker than with the PaK 40, mobility in crew-pull is questioned when only one man of the crew is missing.
> Constructional flaws: The trigger is not pulled by the gunner, but by the crewman 2. This fact affects the accuracy. The gun jumps back after every round fired. The rate of fire is significantly reduced by the necessary re-alignment.

However, both types were regarded as highly effective defensive weapons but considered to be of little value against enemy armour. A combination of weight, poor manoeuvrability and the lack of a suitable gun tractor – many units had received the French-built U-304(f) – made it almost impossible to provide fire support for the advancing infantry. As a result, the command echelon of 377.InfDiv demanded to be equipped with self-propelled guns, and emphasized a preference for the *Sturmgeschütz*.

   In February 1943, the commander of GrRgt 408 (121.InfDiv) delivered a combat report in which he suggested issuing at least two s PaK to each regimental PzJgKp. He dismissed the 5cm PaK since, in his opinion, it was ineffective against the heavily armoured KV-1. He viewed the 3.7cm PaK as an important weapon; lightweight and very manoeuvrable on the battlefield, which he considered as essential for defeating Soviet infantry forces escorting tanks. The gun was also used for destroying any isolated or abandoned tanks. As a result of his report the heavy anti-tank force was issued with the 7.5cm PaK 97/38:

The impact on a target from a hit by high-explosive ammunition fired by a PaK 97/38 is outstanding. Also, both the HL/A and HL/B rounds have proven to be highly effective. However, the shaped-charge round, due to the low velocity, has a maximum effective range of 700m to 800m. Muzzle velocity must be increased to improve accuracy. The lack of tracer-type ammunition is unacceptable. The ammunition boxes, which contain nine rounds, are far too heavy to handle when resupplying guns in front-line positions.

PzSfl 2

On 25 June 1942, six new PzSfl 2 were delivered to 5.PzDiv to equip PzJgAbt 53. The vehicles, transported by rail from Germany, were collected from an

A number of PzSfl 1 were built using the chassis of a PzKpfw II Ausf D and E which had Christie-type suspension; the same as used for the *Flammpanzer* II. But ground clearance was reduced due to the PzSfl 1 being heavier; this caused many problems on the battlefront. The type was armed with a 7.62cm PaK 36(r).

adjacent equipment depot. But there were no trained personnel accompanying the vehicles to provide any operating instructions. during the hand over.

A month later, on 28 July 1942, PzJgAbt 53 submitted an after-action report on the 7.62cm PaK(r) auf PzSfl 2.

Short experience report on 7.62cm PaK(r) auf PzSfl 2

1.) *Panzer-Selbstfahrlafette* 2, (PzKpfw 38[t])
We are still awaiting the delivery of maintenance manuals for the engine, transmission and the running gear. The battalion has experienced no major problems or repairs, only a gearbox which was damaged. However, the tracks are too narrow for operating over marshy terrain; a vehicle frequently becomes bogged down and is almost impossible to recover. Drivers have attempted using maximum power and alternating track drive, but this results in the time-consuming process of adjusting the brake bands.

2.) 7.62cm PaK(r)

The gun barrel travelling rest is too weak and lacks stability. This fault was remedied by our field engineers strengthening the frame. When operating over rough terrain, with the gun barrel released, the elevating gear frequently moved. During training courses at Wünsdorf, all crews reported that the gun had to be adjusted after even the shortest cross-country drive.
Firing trials with the 7.62cm PaK at a stationary KV-1 (up-armoured):

Hull side: 10cm armour – one round of PzGr 39 at 350m range; result a clear penetration.
Turret side: 10cm armour – one round of PzGr 39 at 350m range; result a 20cm long and 3cm deep gouge, no penetration.
Hull front: 10cm armour – one round of PzGr 39 at 150m range, result a clear penetration. The shell passed through the interior and engine compartment before exiting through the rear armour.

In November 1942, PzJgAbt 43 delivered the following report:

Panzerjäger-Abteilung 43
The deployment of the 7.62cm PaK(r) Sfl within II.Armeekorps

Tactical advantages:
The extraordinary advantages of the self-propelled gun are: speed, mobility and

how quickly it can be brought into action. It is advisable for the commander to locate a number of alternative firing positions which can be moved to if necessary; these can be to the rear, since the gun remains accurate even at very long range. All enemy tanks fired at with the PzGr 39, including the heavy KV-1, were defeated. Use of PzGr 40 ammunition was not necessary, consequently only a small quantity was carried in each vehicle. After the few surviving enemy tanks had retreated, the self-propelled guns were deployed to attack troops and artillery positioned in bunkers. The high-explosive ammunition, without delay, was most effective against these targets. But a large number of rounds were consumed, requiring replenishment to be made in the field. Another great advantage was provided by a *Führungspanzer* [command tank], operated by I./PzRgt 10, which enabled radio contact to be maintained throughout the battle. The intercom system in the self-propelled gun was invaluable, since it was necessary for the commander to issue directions to his driver when operating in darkness.

Mechanical advantages:
The [PzKpfw 38(t)] chassis has many good characteristics; easy to drive, highly manoeuvrable and relatively quiet. The vehicle has excellent road

A carefully hidden 7.5cm PaK 40 anti-tank gun effectively strengthens the front-line defences. But the crew would have to be prepared to rapidly change position, since once observed the gun would be targeted by enemy artillery.

A newly delivered Marder II at a railway depot somewhere in the Soviet Union. The vehicle carries markings for 1./PzJgAbt 13 which was an element of 13.PzDiv.

From the very beginning, large numbers of motorcycles and motorcycle combinations had been issued to all units in the *Wehrmacht*. But from 1943, they began to be replaced by the VW Typ 82 *Kübelwagen* (bucket-seat car) or *Typ* 166 *Schwimmwagen* (swimming car).

speed, positive steering and is fitted with a smooth quick-changing gearbox. If the vehicle is driven correctly it is most unlikely that a track would be thrown. But, due to it having a very high profile [silhouette] the gun can be easily spotted by an enemy observer. The commander must always endeavour to keep his vehicle concealed when moving firing positions. In open terrain the vehicle must be carefully positioned because the gun cannot be sufficiently depressed. To avoid the loss of the gun it should be only deployed to fire at targets over 1,000m distant. The gun must never be released from the travelling rest until the firing position is reached; even driving a very short distance without the gun in the rest will seriously affect the preset alignment of the weapon. Consequently, the vehicle would have to be withdrawn for maintenance. No matter how well the vehicle is camouflaged, the first shot fired will reveal its position. This is due to the very large cloud of smoke emitted after firing. For this reason, the gun must be accurately aimed, but the crew must be ready to move the vehicle after a shot has been fired; this should be a frequent operation. In action, unlocking the travel rest is a dangerous task since it requires a member of the crew to clamber up onto the front of the vehicle. Ideally the rest could be unlocked by the driver or radio operator from inside the vehicle.

The crew are not sufficiently protected to the rear or the sides, which means the type can only be safely deployed behind our defensive lines or when escorted by infantry. An increase in the height of the side plates of the gun shield could reduce losses from infantry fire and shrapnel.

The guns cannot be used in woodland because any tree branches within 3m to 4m of the muzzle will cause the HE round to explode; often this will result in injuries to the crew. Where the main gun has an adequate field of fire, the machine gun does not because it is mounted too low and for that reason is seldom used. Also, the vision device for the machine gunner is inadequate, particularly when operating in woodland. Storage space for ammunition on the vehicle is insufficient resulting in guns having to be replenished during an engagement; a dangerous task for supply troops.

Neither the gunner nor the loader has full field of observation since their periscope's field of vision do not cross.

Radio traffic in the firing position is not possible since the enemy can quickly locate the gun and open fire.

Automotive disadvantages:

The long gun barrel leads to an unbalanced centre of gravity, which impairs the leaf springs. Spring and retaining bolts broke frequently. The supply of spare parts was most difficult leading to single guns breaking down for weeks. Greater stocks of spare springs must be provided.

Track ground pressure is too high for driving over marsh-like terrain. Despite being carefully driven, many became stuck and immobilized. A large number had to be abandoned and destroyed by the crew since there were no recovery vehicles.

The lever on the fuel cock, by which the driver changes petrol tanks, is very difficult to actuate and must be modified. Also, the carburettor choke must be re-repositioned since it is almost impossible to use.

Finally, the fuel filler pipe is mounted too deep, causing valuable (and inflammable) petrol to be splashed around and wasted.

As more 7.5cm PaK 40 anti-tank guns became available, a search began to find suitable chassis on which to mount the weapon. One such type selected was the French-built Lorraine *Tracteur Blinde* (armoured tractor) 38L which was designated 7.5cm PaK L/48 *auf Geschützwagen Lorraine-Schlepper* (f) and also known as a Marder I. Production ended in August 1942 after some 170 chassis had been converted. All were delivered with a SdAnh 31 for carrying ammunition.

On 7 December 1942, 290.InfDiv submitted an after-action report:

Experience with the PzKpfw 38(t) chassis mounting the 7.62cm PaK(r)
The division was fortunate to receive six self-propelled guns from 18.InfDiv in time for the attempted a breakthrough by Red Army tanks to the east of Czymanovo.

Experiences:

The type proved to be very effective considering the width of the combat sector covered by the division. Wherever the enemy tanks broke through, the mobile PaK could be rapidly transferred to establish anti-tank defence. Many T-34 tanks fell victim to the powerful gun and ammunition.

The rough terrain and deeply rutted roads, and the weather conditions (snow, ice and frozen slush), hampered the deployment of the self-propelled guns and other vehicles. Many were halted by an engine problem or broken running gear, all of which required time-consuming work to repair. The result was that only 50 per cent of the self-propelled guns were combat ready. However, it can be reported that many of the above problems can be avoided when the type is driven cross-country (avoiding deep snow and steep-sloping terrain) by an experienced or cautious driver.

The height and distinctive profile of the vehicle remains a serious disadvantage. In all instances where a gun has had to be moved from a well-camouflaged position, it has been quickly spotted by an enemy observer and then attacked. Prerequisite for an effective commitment is a brisk driver able to perfectly control the vehicle during a quick change of position under fire.

The ammunition stored in the vehicle is not sufficient to repel a longer tank assault. It is essential to organize an effective supply; stocks of ammunition can be built up when we are in our rear positions. During the battle, four of the six self-propelled guns were lost; three received direct hits from tanks and caught fire and the fourth had an engine failure and had to be blown up.

A carefully camouflaged Marder II has been positioned ready for the launch of *Unternehmen Zitadelle* (Citadel) on the Kursk salient in July 1943. The vehicle is fitted with a 1.4m rod antenna for a *Funksprechgerat* (FuSprGer) 'd' or 'f' transceiver.

Marder II

In September 1942, 4.PzDiv submitted an after-action report:

Experiences regarding the weapon...

These were based on a firing trial using PzGrPatr 39 ammunition and two captured T-34 tanks, positioned at a range of 850m, as a target. A supply of

Above: A PzSfl 1 at a holding position ready for *Unternehmen* Zitadelle. The crew has carefully camouflaged the vehicle to conceal it from being spotted by enemy reconnaissance aircraft. A retractable periscope for the commander is visible behind the gun shield.

Right: An early production Marder II in winter camouflage on the East Front in 1941. The gun mounting required little modification which simplified the production. An SdAnh 31 trailer, carrying extra ammunition, is attached to the vehicle.

both the PzGrPatr 40 and SprGrPatr was not available at that date. The test firing showed that the gun mount is sufficiently stable to withstand recoil loads; the gun carriage was not affected. The breech block and recoil mechanism, recuperator and equalizer all worked faultlessly when eight rounds were fired in rapid succession. The vehicle remained stable at all times. (Trials with the PzGrPatr 40, which has greater gas pressure, await supplies). Adjustments were made after the first round was fired; all subsequent fire was very accurate.

Despite both tanks having received heavy battle damage, it was clearly evident that the PzGrPatr 39 had effectively penetrated the hull and turret on both tanks.

Importantly, the report confirms that neither the PzGrPatr 40 nor the high-explosive round had been supplied to this anti-tank unit fighting on the frontline.

An instructional pamphlet produced by 18.*Armee* provides further interesting detail:

> The commitment of 7.5cm PaK 40 (Sfl Pz II)
>
> 1) The Sfl is designed solely for combat against tanks.
> 2) Due to speed and mobility, the type can be rapidly moved to establish an anti-tank defensive position.
> 3) When enemy tanks attack across a battlefield obscured by trees and bushes, the vehicle can halt the assault by constantly changing position.
> 4) A commitment should never take place in less than in platoon strength; three vehicles.
> 5) A firing position on the upward slope of rising terrain should always be sought.
> 6) Forward reconnaissance is essential and will considerably increase the effectiveness of the type. To avoid the loss of a vehicle in an unclear situation or in particular obscured terrain, the commander should always investigate the area on foot. It is essential that all commanders and NCOs selected have excellent mental agility, are spatially aware and are determined to achieve success.
> 7) Since the self-propelled gun has thin armour, it must never be committed to support an infantry attack or used as an assault gun.
> 8) It is essential for the crew to be allowed sufficient time for daily maintenance of the vehicle and weapons.

Motorized elements of Infantry Division *Grossdeutschland* (InfDiv GD) on the battlefront in 1942. The PzSfl 1 self-propelled anti-tank gun is from the PzJgAbt and the *Sturmgeschütz* (StuG – assault gun) is from the StuGAbt.

PaK 40 (Sfl Pz II), performance data

Weapon: PaK 40
            One MG 34
            One MP 40
            One FuSprech 'f' transceiver

Ammunition:
The ideal provision would be 150 rounds for each gun: 50 SprGrPatr 34, 75 PzGrPatr 38 Hl/B and 25 PzGrPatr 39.

Armour protection:
Chassis 15mm, 11mm superstructure front, 9mm side, 10.5mm gun shield, protects only against infantry fire and shell splinters.

Weight:
11,177kg

Fuel consumption:
This varies from 1.5 litres to 2 litres per km. An hour in combat – short
distances over rough terrain, halted in an ambush or firing position with the
running engine – will consume 40ltr. In a new vehicle, or when an engine
has been replaced, the carburettor will be restricted until it has been run
sufficient hours to operate at full power. During this period fuel consumption
will significantly increase.

The report once again shows that no PzGrPatr 40 had been supplied
and the number of PzGrPatr 39 seems to be somewhat insignificant.
The main ammunition is the PzGrPatr 38 (Hl/B) shaped-charge round.

A damaged Marder II, from an unknown PzJg unit, parked outside a field workshop. In the background is a *Maschinen-Satz* (generator) 'A' mounted on a SdAnh 24 trailer. Note the eight 'kill rings' painted on the gun barrel.

Marder III

In September 1943, the type was in service with PzJgAbt 31 when the unit submitted an after-action report:

Experience gained with PaK Sfl [Marder III] and *Sturmgeschütz...*

When compared to the 7.62cm PaK 36 Sfl 38(t) (120hp Praga engine), the 7.5cm PaK 40 Sfl 38(t) (Praga 180hp engine) has proven to be especially effective and has fulfilled all expectations.

The allotment of PaK Sfl to tank divisions appears, due to the constant lack of new or replacement equipment, somewhat superfluous. However, more should be definitely supplied to infantry divisions.

Reasoning:

The PzKpfw IV in our Panzer divisions can easily defeat enemy armour with their 7.5cm Kwk L/48 gun. But during recent fighting a large number of the self-propelled anti-tank guns issued to Panzer divisions, were committed like tanks. The vehicle was most certainly not intended for this type of deployment and as a consequence, a substantial number were lost.

The size and weight of towed anti-tank guns is increasing and affects manoeuvrability; this makes a rapid move of fire position very difficult. Also, a PaK mot Zug [guns towed by motor vehicles] is virtually impossible to conceal [camouflage] and this causes many problems. As a direct consequence, losses have increased due to attacks by enemy artillery. Despite this we still regard the towed anti-tank gun as an essential weapon for all 14.Kp (infantry/ rifle regiments).

The divisional *Panzerjäger-Abteilung* equipped with the highly mobile self-propelled anti-tank gun can be rapidly withdrawn from the battle, and when necessary be transferred to support forces in other divisional sectors.

As long as it not possible to equip the divisional *Panzerjäger-Abteilungen* with a sufficient number of *Sturmgeschütz*, we consider that it should be supplied with a company of PaK (Sfl) and a company of *Sturmgeschütz*.

Reason

Whereas the self-propelled PaK (Sfl) is poorly armoured, it does have superior optical [sighting and observation] equipment, the *Sturmgeschütz* is lacking in both but is well-armoured. Since it was thought that both types could complement each other on the battlefront, a combined commitment proved to be effective.

The deployment of a tank destroyer unit, even when a unit was up to strength and equipped with the authorized number of weapons, could be affected by many unforeseen problems.

Army regulations required the crews of self-propelled anti-tank guns to be thoroughly trained on how to apply camouflage. Although disguised as a bush, this Marder II would only remain hidden until it opened fire and the resulting cloud of smoke revealed its position.

Right: In May 1942, a new *Geschützwagen* (GW – gun carrier) 38 chassis was designed; the engine was now mounted in the centre of the hull and the gun on the rear. The type was designated Marder III Ausf M armed with a 7.5cm PaK 40/3 anti-tank gun.

Below: The fighting compartment of a Marder III Ausf M provided significantly more space and much easier access for the crew.

Above: A Marder III Ausf M under repair in a workshop near the front. Engineers are using a portable gantry crane to lift the complete gun off the vehicle.

Left: This Marder III Ausf M has received a hit which has penetrated the superstructure and exploded in the engine compartment. Note, the MG 34 in an anti-aircraft mounting fitted on the gun shield.

At the end of 1942, the combat strength of PzJgAbt 616, attached to *Heeresgruppe Mitte*, had been severely depleted in recent fighting. To compensate for the losses, the unit received replacement equipment from 4.PzDiv and 18.PzDiv.

In March 1943, PzJgAbt 616 delivered an experience report:

> On 21 January 1943, the battalion received the following from 4.PzDiv and 18.PzDiv:
>
> – 18 7.62cm PaK 36 auf *Fahrgestell* [Fgst – chassis] 38(t)
> – Three 7.5cm PaK 40 auf Fgst PzKpfw II

A Marder II camouflaged under debris from damaged buildings. Although an anti-tank gun, the 7.5cm PaK 40 was very effective against buildings, when firing high-explosive ammunition.

The material was delivered to us at Kastornoie, but it was found that six of the Sfl from 18.PzDiv were not operational. Also, during the transfer the delivery personnel were not able to thoroughly explain the workings of self-propelled guns. Furthermore, no operating or servicing manuals for the engine, transmission, running gear and the weapon were handed over.

The servicing of the PzKpfw 38(t) chassis and engine, particularly the clutch and gearbox [transmission], was a difficult task for our workshop engineers since they had not received any training on the type. Even the delivery team was unable to provide any instructions to our personnel. The amount of spare parts supplied was totally insufficient and it would be impossible to acquire these parts from other sources. Also, special servicing tools were not supplied. Finally, our request for a Škoda specialist engineer was rejected.

When the battalion was sent into combat at Gorshetshno on 25 January 1943, our engineers had received only three days of instruction on the chassis and ordnance. This left us with no time to sufficiently train the drivers and gun crews.

During the first combat operations a disproportionate number (11) of self-propelled guns failed due to mechanical problems, and had to be blown up by the crews:

Seven with a damaged clutch
One with a damaged gearbox
One with a damaged cooling system
Two with a jammed breech block

The majority of these losses were caused by minor problems and would have been avoidable if our engineers had received proper training or were supplied with adequate spare parts. The situation was further exacerbated by the

A newly delivered Marder II painted in standard *dunkelgrau* (dark grey) in service with a replacement and training battalion. These units were equipped to provide the most comprehensive training possible.

inadequate instruction received by the drivers. This lack also applied to the gun crew; during the first mission against tanks, the guns on three Sfl were incorrectly adjusted, which resulted in the total loss of the vehicles. Significantly, one gun hit its target with the seventh round fired.

Ammunition

Possibly because Germany had limited natural resources, the government and military planners decided to make a significant investment in the development of advanced more powerful weapons and ammunition. One example is the 7.5cm PaK 41 which was designed as a very high velocity (1,260mps) anti-tank gun with a formidable armour penetration performance (130mm armour at 1,000m range) when firing 7.5cm PzGrPatr 41 *Hartkern* (Hk – solid core, tungsten carbide) ammunition. But availability was never guaranteed due to a constant shortage of tungsten carbide, forcing military planners to order the development of the 7.5cm PzGrPatr 41 *Stahlkern* (StK– hardened steel).

Far left: A whitewashed Marder III Ausf M from PzJgAbt 251: Note badge of the unit has been stencilled on the superstructure. Also, that the driver's position is protected by a cast metal item rather than being fabricated from welded armour plates.

Below: The crew of a Marder II at a loading area. German units used rail transport wherever possible, even for relatively short distances, to preserve the engine, transmission and running gear of their tracked vehicles.

Several German documents produced during the war state that penetration data for both types of ammunition as being identical – an implausibility that cannot be explained.

In July 1942, a short time after introduction of the various types of s PaK, the supply echelon of VII.*Armeekommando* sent a questionnaire out to all attached PzJgAbt:

> The 7.5cm PzGr 39 [a conventional armour-piercing round available for PaK 40 and PaK 36(r)] can defeat virtually all heavy Soviet tanks (Matilda, T-34 and KV-1) at up to 1,200m range; under favourable conditions 1,600m range is possible. When fired from the 7.62cm Russian-PaK, impact performance is almost identical.
>
> The 7.5cm GrPatr 38 Hl/B [shaped-charge round] for the 7.5cm PaK 97/38 is clearly inferior, and is only effective up to 900m range. A KV-1 *verstärkt* (appliqué armour) was engaged at 400m and 19 rounds were fired. Hits were observed on the hull and side of the turret, but the tank was not halted.
>
> The PzGr 40 high-velocity, armour-piercing ammunition fired by the 5cm PaK 38 could, at a favourable angle of impact, penetrate the turret and rear armour on a KV-1 Model 1942 at 80m range. A 5cm PzGr 39 was not at all effective. However, the 5cm SprGrPatr 38 high-explosive ammunition was very effective when used against infantry targets.

At the date the report was written, it appears that PzGr 40 ammunition was not available for the 7.5cm PaK 40. The round had very high penetration performance at short and medium range, but this decreased significantly at ranges over 1,200m. However, the ever-present shortage of tungsten caused this ammunition to be supplied in very limited quantities. As an alternative, crews were directed to use the 7.5cm PzGr 39 or the 7.5cm GrPatr 38 Hl/B.

The shortage caused a variant of the 7.5cm PzGrPatr 40, without a tungsten core, to be developed: The 7.5cm PzGrPatr 40 *Weicheisen* (W – soft iron). This round was significantly inferior to the PzGrPatr 39, and of course PzGrPatr 40 Hk. As noted in a document, the round was only produced to keep open the production facilities manufacturing the PzGrPatr 40 Hk.

Due to the PaK 38 anti-tank gun being obviously ineffective, all the units questioned unanimously agreed that it should be replaced by the 7.5cm PaK 40.

A training pamphlet (MB 47b/35), provided detailed instructions of how to use the different types of ammunition, but the gun commander had to make the ultimate choice depending on the type of tank and combat range. In reality, the PzGrPatr 39 was to be used against all tank types and pillboxes at up to 1,500m range; in exceptional cases up to 1,800m, whereas the PzGrPatr 40 was only to be used to defeat difficult-to-destroy heavy tanks. But due to the loss of ballistic performance, over longer distances, the maximum recommended combat range was 1,000m. Anti-tank units on the battlefront were ordered to conserve their supply of PzGrPatr 40 Hk and only fire at a carefully selected target.

The equipment on every tank destroyer, including a Marder II, included a 7.92mm *Machinengewehr* (MG – machine gun) 34 for use as a self-defence weapon.

The part-armoured SdKfz 11/1 normally mounted a 2cm FlaK 38 as a self-propelled anti-aircraft gun. Here a *Panzerjäger* unit has utilized one, without a FlaK 38, as the towing vehicle for a 7.5cm PaK 40.

If the PzGrPatr 39 was not available, then the PzGrPatr 38 (Hl/B and Hl/C) was to be used for defeating all types of armour and heavily armoured tanks. The round was effective at up to 1,200m range.

However, there are clear discrepancies between the questionnaire for the Marder II and the instruction pamphlet.

The high-explosive SprGrPatr 34, with or without a delay fuse, could be used at ranges from 2,800m to 5,200m. Maximum range, if the gun was fitted with an *Aushilfsrichtmittel* (auxiliary gun-laying device) 38, was 7,700m.

Although the above applies to the 7.5cm PaK 40 anti-tank gun, the different types of ammunition were available for most types of anti-tank gun in service with German forces, including the 3.7cm PaK, the 4.7cm PaK(t), the 5cm PaK 38 and the 7.62cm PaK 36. But, the 7.5cm PaK 97/38 and the 7.5cm PaK 41 were an exception and required dedicated ammunition.

A large number of after-action reports, written in early 1943, show that the s PaK – in particular the 7.62cm PaK 36 and 7.5cm PaK 40 – was the standard gun in service with all front-line *Panzerjäger* units.

Since the development of more powerful anti-tank weapons had been initiated, front-line forces would survive the perilous situation they faced at the end of 1941.

However, all towed anti-tank guns were affected by the same operational problems.

- Mobility was dependent on the availability of suitable motor vehicles [tractors].
- It was time consuming, often due to battlefield conditions, to get the gun into a ready-to-fire position.
- Protection against enemy fire and shrapnel was totally inadequate resulting in the loss of many battle-experienced crewmen.

In 1943, the German advance on the Eastern Front had been halted; in the south 6.*Armee* was surrounded and fighting for survival at Stalingrad. *Heeresgruppe Mitte* and *Heeresgruppe Nord* were managing to hold their positions despite being under heavy attack by the Red Army, which appeared to have an endless supply of manpower and replacement equipment. Here their tank units, most equipped with the T-34, were deployed in large formations (followed by infantry) and played a decisive part in the outcome of the battle.

In February 1943, a specialist officer from AOK 18 (*Heeresgruppe Nord*) was ordered to evaluate anti-tank defences in the east. As a result, he produced *Panzerabwehr-Erfahrungen* an extensive report in which he indentified the shortcomings of a purely offensive anti-tank force. The *Panzerjäger* had to face reality:

Anti-tank Defence

1.) Leadership

The leadership was forced to distribute its limited tank destroyer resources to defend against an enemy who succeeded in making simultaneous massed tank attacks. Because of the severe winter frost, the enemy was able to advance over the many frozen-solid swamp or water obstacles which had previously been impassable. Furthermore, the thick covering of frozen snow reduced the effectiveness of our many minefields. Under these circumstances, despite the long distances and fragile communication lines, the army was called on for support. Anti-tank reserves, essential for the establishment of defensive strong points, were organized and their deployment thoroughly planned. After making an assessment of all units, and the overall situation, a situation map was produced to show the location of all available types of anti-tank weapon.

These were listed by calibre and branch of service – PaK mot-Z and Sfl, 8.8cm FlaK, StuG and Panzer.

Other preparations included locating approach routes for the rapid movement reserves and weapons, field reconnaissance units were deployed and lines of communication commands established.

2.) Weapons

a) PzJg and FlaK

The mobility of the medium and heavy PaK suffered from the lack of suitable all-terrain tractors. Even the army could only keep moving its PaK and FlaK reserves during combat, by establishing dedicated units equipped with tractors. The number of s PaK was insufficient at beginning of the deployment and decreased further as losses mounted. Fortunately, at the end of January large numbers of s PaK (mot and Sfl) were being delivered to the army. But crews were required for the self-propelled guns, and training them would be very time consuming. The result was that on an average just ten s PaK were available for

A Marder II in service with a *Luftwaffe* field division carries an interesting camouflage scheme; the dark yellow base colour is almost covered over with large patches of olive green.

each division. A number of FlaK units were frequently used in the anti-tank role. Nowhere on the frozen terrain was impassable for enemy tanks, which forced commanders to position the s PaK directly in the frontline. The distinctively high outline of the 8.8cm FlaK and 7.62cm PaK required them to be placed in staggered positions some distance behind the frontline.

Many of the divisions are equipped with the 7.5cm PaK 97/38. But when fighting in woodland a number of accidents (many fatal) occurred, due to the shaped-charge ammunition being highly-sensitive, often exploding after hitting a small branch.

Anti-tank combat teams were called on to destroy any of our tanks which had been immobilized, but were still able to fire.

By concentrating our anti-tank weapons our troops had destroyed a total of 400 enemy tanks. But it has to be remembered that this score was achieved by a relatively small number of weapons. For instance, the 8.8cm FlaK guns destroyed 47 enemy tanks.

b) *Sturmgeschütz*

Once again, the assault gun has proven to be the most mobile *Panzerjäger*, particularly when when deployed at focal points. As an example, from 13 January to 31 March 1943, StuGAbt 226 destroyed a total of 210 enemy tanks. In contrast, the five StuG batteries of *Luftwaffe* field units destroyed 17 enemy tanks.

c) Tanks

The enemy had nothing comparable to the PzKpfw VI [Tiger], but there were never more than four of the type in action on the battlefront; Tigers from 1./s PzAbt 502 destroyed over 160 enemy tanks. A thorough reconnaissance of the battlefront, although a difficult and hazardous task, was essential to allow our forces to be effectively deployed to defeat any enemy assault and keep our casualty count to a minimum. The substantial network of railways behind the front was a great benefit for all combat operations beyond 50km allowing the movement of men and equipment without concern for weak bridges, poor road surfaces and, most importantly, consumption of fuel.

The success of the *Sturmgeschütz* and the PzKpfw IV cannot be overstated, since Soviet tanks have far superior cross-country mobility.

The report provides some detail of the dire situation faced by many units of the German army on the Eastern Front. The replacement of ineffective towed anti-tank guns with improved, more powerful weapons had been initiated and was progressing. But front-line troops had clear priorities, although the self-propelled PaK had all the attributes required for mobile warfare it did lack sufficient armour protection for the crew. In the eyes of the struggling infantry the perfect weapon was the *Sturmgeschütz*.

In February 1943, all independent *Heeres-Panzerjäger* units in 18.*Armee* were entirely equipped with either the towed or self-propelled s PaK. In a battle, these units would be used to reinforce anti-tank defences. The self-propelled s PaK was sometimes deployed as a replacement *Sturmgeschütz* unit or even a tank unit, to allow both of the latter to be available for other missions. But this was only done for limited periods during defensive fighting.

On 4 February 1943, a strength report was delivered by 383.InfDiv:

a) Infantry

Nine battalions, of which six are combat ready and three are nearing combat readiness.

Six of these battalions are fully mobile and three are some 40 per cent mobile.

b) Winter mobile infantry

One medium strength Ski battalion (winter mobile) and two Ski-Kp from 45.InfDiv.

The vehicle on the left is a production Marder II. The vehicle in the centre is a PzKpfw II mounting a 5cm PaK 38, but appears to be awaiting repair. On the right is a PzKpfw II mounting a complete, less wheels, 7.5cm PaK 40 anti-tank gun.

c) Artillery

Six light batteries, three heavy batteries, two *Nebelwerfer* batteries, all are fully mobile, some are horse drawn.

Bodenständige Beutegeschütze [captured guns/rocket launchers]:

Two FK 7.65cm (j – Yugoslavian)

Ten FK 8.76cm (e – English)

Three 12.2cm(r) field guns

Two 12.2cm(r) howitzers

14 heavy Wurfgeräte 40

Attached units:

Heeres-FlaK-Abt 273

One heavy battery of four 8.8cm FlaK and three 2cm FlaK

One light battery with nine 2cm guns and two 2cm FlaK-Vierling

d) Tank destroyer elements

20 5cm PaK: Three fully motorized, five temporarily motorized and 12 are horse drawn.

Eight 7.5cm PaK 40; motorized.

22 7.5cm PaK 97/38: two motorized, 20 are without tractors and also lack sighting telescopes.

e) Attached tank destroyer elements:

2./PzJgAbt 45 with seven 7.5cm PaK 97/38 and tractors.

The report shows an infantry unit operating with a wide range of equipment: importantly the artillery element appears to be poorly equipped, except for a few German rocket launchers. Interestingly, beside the two captured Yugoslavian field guns (FK 7.65cm[j]) the unit was supplied with 20 British Ordnance QF 25 pounders (FK 8.76cm[e]). Conversely, the unit appears to have a sufficient number of anti-tank guns, but only eight 7.5cm PaK 40 high-performance guns are noted; otherwise there are twenty 5cm PaK 38 and 22 ex-French 7.5cm PaK 97/38. The 3.7cm PaK is not mentioned since it was deemed to be obsolete. An even more serious problem was a lack of effective mobility; a large number of anti-tank guns were horse drawn, and nothing was available to tow the majority of PaK 97/38. Finally, it seems strange that a number of guns lacked sighting telescopes.

More Mobility Problems

In September 1943, more than a year after the first s PaK had been issued to German units, 267.InfDiv submitted an experience report to AOK 18:

When faced by a major enemy assault it is a proven fact that their tanks must be prevented from penetrating our lines. Ideally, the enemy attack must be stopped as they leave the cover of their own front-line positions. Fortunately, the division had placed a number of s PaK in an area near our front-line positions; a successful deployment. It is essential that these valuable weapons are positioned so they are not vulnerable to attack by enemy artillery. Ideally the guns should be positioned in shelters built to withstand a direct hit by a 12.2cm shell fired by Soviet artillery. However, moving the gun out of the shelter into position, even over firm ground, would be not only impossible but also impractical. The 7.5cm PaK 97/38 weighs 1,320kg, the 7.62cm PaK 36 over 1,727kg, to the 8.5cm FlaK(r) some 3,048kg; even a crew of eight very strong men would have problems moving any of the above.

A means of towing is essential to the deployment of the heavy PaK; the best firing position is worth nothing if the gun cannot be moved to it quickly. The large gun must not be positioned on an open road or near a junction, since these are preferred targets for enemy artillery to strike. But to move the s PaK

The more powerful SdKfz 11 half-track tractor was more suitable for towing a heavy anti-tank gun – here a 7.62cm PaK 39(r) – than the SdKfz 10. An additional benefit was that the type had more room for the gun crew and also space for ammunition.

into position off-road, an all-terrain tractor is an essential requirement. The division has the following types for towing duties:

- Six Somua MCG 5 half-track tractors, towing capacity approximately 5,080kg and suitable for the 7.62cm PaK (replacing the SdKfz 11).
- Two Hanomag K 50 tracked tractor, towing capacity approximately 5,080kg and suitable for the 8.5cm FlaK(r) (replacing the SdKfz 6).
- Three Vickers-Armstrong 601 tracked tractors, towing capacity 1,016kg, suitable for the 4.5cm PaK(r) (replacing the Kfz 69).
- Three Lanz-Bulldog T 9500 agricultural tractor, towing capacity 3,050kg and suitable for the 7.5cm and 7.62cm PaK (replacing SdKfz 10 and SdKfz 11).
- Seven Krupp-built Kfz 69 for towing 2cm FlaK.
- Four SdKfz 10 issued on 31 March 1943 for towing the 7.5cm PaK.

With the exception of the recently issued SdKfz 10, these (above) tractors certainly do not meet our requirements. The loss of an s PaK on 29 March, at Bolshaja Kamenka, was definitely due to the lack of a suitable towing vehicle. Tank destroyer units require a tractor which should almost be soundless when running and have excellent cross-country mobility. Also, it should have sufficient room for the crew, their personal gear and weapons but also anti-tank ammunition.

We request supply of the SdKfz 10 for towing the 7.5cm PaK 40, and also the SdKfz 11 to tow the 7.62cm PaK 36(r).

The supply of ammunition will remain a problem. Additional all-terrain ammunition trucks will be needed.

This report submitted by 267.InfDiv illustrates the dramatic reality faced by anti-tank forces on the Eastern Front. Although the unit was issued with the usual 7.5cm PaK 40 and 7.62cm PaK 36(r) guns, neither the 3.7cm PaK nor 5cm PaK 38 are mentioned, which indicates that it refers only to the divisional PzJgAbt and not to the anti-tank weapons held by infantry regiments. Like many other units awaiting deliveries of new or replacement weapons, the division was forced to utilize integrated captured weapons such as the Russian-built 4.5cm PaK(r) or 8.5cm FlaK(r), but this caused many logistical problems.

More serious was the complete lack of suitable gun tractors. The unit had been supplied with captured French, Belgian and British vehicles; even a number of German-built agricultural tractors (Hanomag or Lanz). But what it desperately required to operate effectively was a sufficient number of the highly efficient SdKfz 10 and SdKfz 11 half-track tractors. The anti-aircraft section in the PzJgAbt was equipped with a 2cm FlaK towed by Krupp (Kfz 69) Protze tractors.

The wishful thinking expressed by the divisional commander for a gun tractor which had excellent road and cross-country towing performance – also room to carry a gun crew and ammunition – is understandable. However, a new type of half-track vehicle (ordered by Hitler in 1942) was designed and developed by Bussing-NAG which, in principle, fulfilled his wishes. Designated the *Schwerer Wehrmachtsschlepper* (SWS – heavy military tractor) the type entered service in 1944, but production was slow and only some 820 had been delivered by the end of the war.

In 1943, German military planners indicated that they considered the *Sturmgeschütz* and self-propelled anti-tank and artillery guns to be far superior weapons.

The self-propelled anti-tank gun – here a PzSfl 1 – was best deployed to take full advantage of the long-range weapons they carried.

Both: The PzKpfw 38(t) chassis was considerably modified for the Marder III Ausf M. The engine was moved forward from the rear compartment and position next to the driver. This allowed a lower floor to be fitted for the gun mounting, which in turn provided more protection for the crew. The vehicle was powered by a 7,754cc Praga *Typ* TNHPS six-cylinder water-cooled petrol engine. The vehicle was designated SdKfz 139.

Both: An unchanged PzKpfw 38(t) chassis was utilized for the Marder III Ausf H but with the turret removed. The gun was mounted in what had been a fighting compartment, which only had space for the gunner and loader. The vehicle was fitted the Praga *Typ* TNHPS petrol engine, as fitted in the Ausf M, and was designated SdKfz 138.

The instigation of the s PaK programme in 1942 marked an important turning point for the *Panzerjäger*. Orders were issued to the armaments industry in the Reich to design, develop and manufacture 7.5cm [resp 7.62cm] anti-tank guns: German tank destroyer units were to be supplied weapons sufficiently powerful to defeat the latest types of Russian tank encountered during *Unternehmen* Barbarossa.

German military planners were aware that the shortage would be a constant problem, since it was obvious to them that the manufacturers were unable to produce the required numbers. As a result, they ordered (influenced by Hitler) that German forces were to utilize any operable anti-tank guns – and other equipment – captured from or abandoned by the retreating Red Army.

The *Fremde Heere Ost* (intelligence department foreign armies: East) after failing to acknowledge that the Red Army had a number of modern tanks before the launch of *Unternehmen* Barbarossa in 1941, apparently became more cautious in 1942. While the introduction of sophisticated German anti-tank guns and tanks was under way, officials from the department were alert for any new information, regarding Soviet armour, when a report was delivered, noting that the Red Army had a new, heavily armed and amoured tank that was about to appear on the battlefront. The report was a complete fallacy, possibly originated by deliberate false statements made by Russian prisoners of war (PoW) undergoing interrogation; several spoke of a 'multi-turreted 100-ton tank'.

Although military planners in Germany had already ordered the design, development and production of battlefield-superior PzKpfw VI Tiger heavy

The 8.8cm PaK 43/1 L/71 *auf Geschützwagen* III/ IV was designed by Alkett and utilized components, as the designation suggests, from a PzKpfw III and a PzKpfw IV. The type mounted the formidable 8.8cm PaK 43/1 anti-tank gun which, in ideal conditions, could defeat an M4 Sherman at over 2,500m range. It was first known as *Hornisse* (hornet) but Adolf Hitler soon ordered this to be changed to *Nashorn* (rhinoceros). Here two of the type, from s PzJgAbt 525, are deploying to the Nettuno bridgehead.

In 1942, the 7.5cm KwK 42 L/70 was available for installation in the new PzKpfw V Panther medium tank. The high-performance gun was also intended to be to supplied to anti-tank units as the 7.5cm PaK 44. Here Adolf Hitler examines an experimental self-propelled gun mounting the same weapon on a semi-armoured SdKfz 11 half-track tractor.

tank and the PzKpfw V Panther medium tank, they had also initiated work on a number of more powerful tanks for the future – PzKpfw VI Tiger II (B): PzKpfw E 100 and the super-heavy Porsche *Typ* 205 *Maus* (mouse). Another measure taken was to accelerate the up-gunning of types already in service.

The planners applied the same logic in regard to new equipment for German anti-tank forces. At the same time as the latest s PaK (7.5cm PaK 41, 7.5cm PaK 40, 7.62cm PaK 36(r) and 7.5cm Pak 97/38) were entering service, *Waffenprüfamt* (WaPrüf – weapon development and testing department) 4 continued to issue contracts for companies to design even more effective weapons.

7.5cm PaK 44

The ballistic performance of the 7.5cm KwK 42, being developed for the new PzKpfw V Panther, was improved by lengthening the gun barrel to improve muzzle velocity. Designated 7.5cm KwK 42 L/70 the gun was capable of penetrating armour 140mm thick at a range of 1,000m when firing conventional anti-tank ammunition.

The KwK 42 was used for the 7.5cm PaK 42 anti-tank gun, but little is known as to whether it was produced in any numbers or even if it entered front-line service. However, in September 1942 the weapon was shown to

Adolf Hitler and *Rüstungsminister* (armaments minister) Albert Speer who demanded that development work should be continued, but he was adamant that the gun barrel length (calibre) must be increased to L/100 and preferably L/120. If firing trials were successful, then he saw no reason why the calibres should not be further increased while ignoring the service life of the gun barrel and accuracy.

Fortunately, his somewhat naive demands were ignored or conveniently forgotten. Priority was now given to developing the 8.8cm FlaK as an anti-tank gun.

8.8cm PaK L/71

In the first few months of World War II, WaPrüf 10 ordered the development of a new anti-aircraft gun. The existing 8.8cm FlaK 36 gun had a maximum vertical firing range of 10,500m, which the department decided was completely was inadequate. As a result, three manufacturers – Rheinmetall-Borsig, Krupp and Škoda – were each issued with a contract to design and develop a replacement.

The production contract for the new 8.8cm FlaK gun was issued to Rheinmetall-Borsig, but with the proviso that they utilized the two-part barrel construction designed by Krupp. Designated 8.8cm FlaK 41, the gun

Although the 7.5cm Kwk 44 L/70 had an excellent performance, Hitler would continue to demand even more increases without any regard to the service life of the gun barrel. Also, the weapon on this vehicle was designed to be lifted off and mounted on a simple cruciform-type carriage; an interesting approach to creating an economical self-propelled or basic anti-tank gun. The type remained experimental.

The first 400 of the 8.8cm PaK 43 delivered to anti-tank units had a cruciform-type carriage mounted on an SdAnh 204 two-axle trailer.

would become one of the most effective anti-aircraft weapons in service during World War II. When compared to the FlaK 36, vertical range was significantly increased to 14,600m, but the weapon was considerably heavier and the service life of the gun barrel reduced from 5,000 rounds to 1,000.

On 4 June 1942, a *Rüstungs-Besprechung* (armaments meeting) was held to discuss making improvements to a number of German anti-tank guns. Hitler, who attended the meeting, had been made aware that the FlaK 41 had an excellent ballistic performance and demanded:

> 36.) The Führer orders the immediate development of an 8.8cm PaK based on the 8.8cm FlaK 41.

A month later Hitler intervened again, demanding that development of the new anti-tank gun must be accelerated and, now that mobility was finally being taken seriously, the type should be either vehicle towed or mounted as a self-propelled gun.

In September 1942, Hitler again insisted that work on the new gun must be accelerated. But production of the gun carriage was delayed by numerous unresolved problems.

Notes from a Führer-Besprechung held on 9 September:

33.) 8.8cm PaK 43 (mot)

Production of the various final versions developed from the 8.8cm PaK 43 will not be possible by spring 1943. For this reason, we urgently need to determine which motor vehicle or self-propelled carriage, which is currently in production, is suitable for towing or mounting the 8.8cm PaK 43. Some 400 to 500 will have to be delivered by 12 May 1943. It is vital that a decision is made on the final three solutions currently being developed.

34.) Gun on self-propelled carriage

Since the projected le FH 43 (on self-propelled carriage) will be a completely new type, other available chassis must be developed as trials vehicles. Rheinmetall and Krupp have suggested that it could be useful to build one example of an 8.8cm PaK 43 mounted on the chassis of the le FH 43 (Sfl).

The above shows that all design, development and pre-production work on the gun had been completed by September, but problems remained with the carriage and no decision had been made on a chassis for the self-propelled version.

Krupp was selected to produce the 8.8cm PaK and decided to mount it on a new type of cruciform-shaped carriage, similar to that used the medium FlaK gun, to allow an all-round field of fire. On 14 October, representatives from Krupp reported to Hitler that all preliminary work on their 8.8cm PaK

The continuing shortage of towing tractors caused many, especially training, units to relinquish most of their allotted vehicles to keep units equipped with the new 8.8cm PaK 43 mobile. Pioneer units in particular lost most of their SdKfz 6 medium half-track tractors and others lost their 4.5-ton *Maultier* (mule) half-track trucks.

was completed and the company had been authorized to begin production, with the first gun being available for firing trials in December. Hitler again emphasized the importance of the production schedule, but he possibly realized that it would never be achieved.

Facing problems with the manufacture of carriages, it was even suggested to use those from captured Soviet 122mm artillery pieces. But again, Hitler intervened since he thought that these *Beutewaffen* (captured weapons) should be held in reserve to replace any 10.5cm le FH 18 or the heavy 10cm K 18 lost in action. Rheinmetall-Borsig, Krupp and Škoda were all instructed to create a finalized design that could be produced in the required quantities and on time – 500 by 12 May 1943. However, none of this work should be allowed affect any equipment then in the process of being manufactured.

The proposal to produce a self-propelled carriage mounting the le FH 43 (Sfl) was still at the project stage and it became obvious in the summer of 1942 that it would never be built. An interim solution was urgently sought and Alkett, a specialist tracked-vehicle producer, was contracted to develop a vehicle assembled only from readily-available components.

8.8cm PaK 43/41

For reasons unknown, the Krupp-built PaK 43 was late entering production making the target, 500 guns by May 1943, impossible to meet. This resulted in a number of major alterations.

The constant lack of suitable half-track tractors forced anti-tank units to improvise. Here a team of six horses has been harnessed to an 8.8cm PaK 43/41 so that it can be repositioned.

The decision was taken to utilize the upper carriage and lower split-type carriage as used on the Rheinmetall-designed 10cm K 41; the proposed replacement for the le FH 18, which never entered service. Fortunately, the design of a number of items had been finalized and these were ready for production. The gun barrel had a horizontal sliding-type breech block attached to a conventional cradle for mounting on the new type of carriage. However, from the beginning this was intended to only be an interim solution.

The new weapon was designated 8.8cm PaK 43/41, the suffix 41 indicates to the use of the K 41 carriage.

The 3.7cm PaK first entered service in 1933 and just ten years' production of the formidable high-performance 8.8cm PaK 43 began. But development of the gun carriage had not been completed, which meant utilizing the split-trail type for the proposed 10cm K 41 field gun.

8.8cm PaK 43

On 5 January 1943, Krupp presented a wooden mock-up of their proposed 8.8cm PaK to officials at a *Rüstungs-Besprechung*. The gun was not carried on a conventional split-trail carriage, but was mounted on a cruciform-type carriage similar to that of the medium FlaK gun. In February 1943, Hitler issued an order for the production of the new Krupp anti-tank gun to commence, but only after the first series of 500 guns had been completed. He also issued another order for a number of the type to be delivered to the *Heerestruppen-Artillerie* (army artillery), and fitted with suitable advanced sighting and observation telescopes.

The crew of a 7.5cm PaK 40 prepare for action. The commander kneels to the left of the gun, while K1 (gunner) and K2 (loader) crouch in their positions behind the gun shield; K3 and K4 (general crew) put their weight on the trails. (Getty)

8.8cm PaK 43/41

Calibre	8.8cm
Barrel length	6,580mm = L/71
Range (maximum)	14,200m (HE)
Muzzle velocity	1,140mps (PzGr 40)
Height of muzzle	1,270mm
Traverse	56 degrees
Elevation	-5 degrees to +38 degrees
Rate of fire	6–10rpm
Weight	400kg
Armour penetration 100m	250mm (PzGr 40)
Armour penetration 1,000m	193mm
Armour penetration 1,500m	170mm
Armour penetration 4,000m	80mm

8.8cm PaK 43

Calibre	8.8cm
Barrel length	6,585mm = L/71
Range (maximum)	14,200m (HE)
Muzzle velocity	1,140mps (PzGr 40)
Height of muzzle	1,100mm
Traverse	360 degrees
Elevation	-8 degrees to +40 degrees
Rate of fire	6–10rpm
Weight (travelling)	5,400kg
Weight (in action)	3,760kg
Armour penetration 100m	250mm (PzGr 40)
Armour penetration 1,000m	193mm
Armour penetration 1,500m	170mm
Armour penetration 4,000m	80mm

The Krupp-designed PaK 43 was of conventional design, but was fitted with a drop-block breech mechanism and used a jacket-type cradle to facilitate easier loading and handling.

The initial 400 built were mounted on a two-axle SdAnh 204. A simplified trailer, carried on steel wheels fitted with solid rubber tyres, later became standard equipment.

In an emergency situation the gun could be fired directly from the trailer, but only if the side trails were folded out for support; theoretically, an all-round field of fire was possible. The crew was protected from infantry fire and shrapnel by a large sloped-armour gun shield.

When used in the artillery role against long-range targets, it was vital to use the cruciform mounting.

In October 1943, a first assessment was given during a presentation to the Führer:

a) The 8.8cm PaK 43 in its current two-axle version is a highly satisfactory anti-tank gun capable of opening fire, almost instantly, from the trailer. The gun has an all-round field of fire and can be elevated up to 40 degrees.

b) The 8.8cm PaK 43/41 (split trail carriage) must preferably be positioned in a bunker due to its inadequate mobility.

Far left: Minister of Armaments Albert Speer often organized demonstrations of the weapons being developed by the German armaments industry. Many were attended by Adolf Hitler; here inspecting different types of anti-tank ammunition.

Below: An 8.8cm PaK 43/41 in an open firing position protecting a road junction in Russian city. Note the spades have not been dug-in to prevent the recoil from throwing the gun backwards.

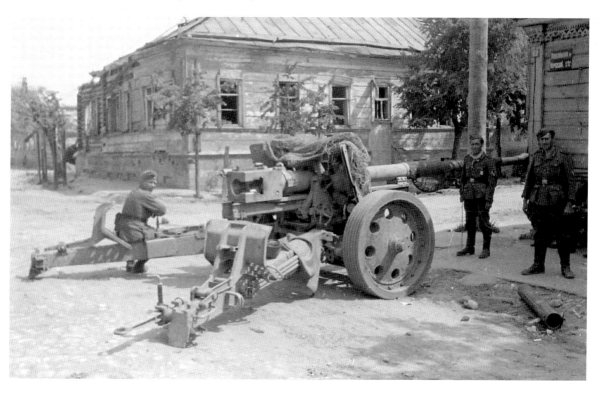

Production of 8.8cm PaK 43/41 and PaK 43

The *Rüststand* table of statistics, prepared by the ministry of armaments and munitions, provides reliable data for the production of the 8.8cm PaK 43/41, 8.8cm PaK 43 and also the *schwerer Panzerjäger* (s PzJg – heavy tank destroyer) *Hornisse* (hornet).

The planned delivery of 500 PaK 43/41 was achieved in May 1943, and were allocated as follows:

	PaK 43/41	PaK 43	Towed PaK combined		s PzJg *Hornisse/Nashorn*		
8.8cm PaK L/71, all versions							
	Built	Built	Front losses	Available	Built	Front losses	Available
February 1943	1	0	0	0	14	0	6
March 1943	23	0	0	4	30	0	31
April 1943	112	0	0	111	41	0	73
May 1943	267	0	0	391	35	0	110
June 1943	80	0	0	461	35	5	131
July 1943	70	0	47	421	44	4	173
August 1943	61	0	69	378	16	19	179
September 1943	55	0	8	433	27	5	180
October 1943	67	0	17	472	42	16	211
November 1943	40	0	12	486	24	1	211
December 1943	80	6	30	458	37	17	250
January 1944	31	0	32	469	0	17	263
February 1944	31	139	54	536	25	25	261
March 1944	58	104	8	682	0	32	248
April 1944	40	103	21	741	20	10	230
May 1944	40	121	7	847	24	7	225
June 1944	40	136	16	1,004	6	48	238
July 1944	6	174	53	1,144	3	34	216
August 1944	5	176	219	1,125	31	20	191
September 1944	0	165	94	578	12	0	147
October 1944	0	200	46	674	7	7	129
November 1944	0	216	157	707	5	0	139
December 1944	0	232	31	705	0	4	159
January 1945	0	115	52	829	12	20	155
February 1945	0	132	56	1,017	3	?	141
March 1945	0	75	?	1,184	1	?	?
	1,107	2,094	1,029	-	494	291	-

- 300 PaK 43/41 for units on the Eastern Front.
- 100 PaK 43/41 for units stationed or refurbished in the west.
- 100 PaK 43/41 as self-propelled guns issued to s PzJgAbt [heavy tank destroyer battalion] 560 and PzJgAbt 655.

A 7.5cm PaK 40 and an 8.8cm PaK 43/41 being prepared for action at a training establishment. To save anti-tank ammunition, both guns have been fitted with a 7.92mm MG 34 loaded with tracer ammunition to allow the gunner to observe trajectory and hits on the target.

Organization

The 8.8cm PaK in its various configurations (PaK 43/41, PaK 43 and PaK 43/1 *Hornisse*) were primarily issued to anti-tank units at *Heerestruppen* (army troop) level, but there were some exceptions. Due to the gun having a good ballistic performance, it was supplied to a number of artillery units and deployed as a heavy field gun. The type was also supplied to a number of *Festungs-PaK* units which had been established in defensive fortifications around some cities in the east.

Army Anti-tank Battalions

Units in *Heeres Panzerjäger-Abteilungen* (H PzJgAbt – army anti-tank battalions) were issued with the best anti-tank guns available.

As an example, H PzJgAbt (8.8cm) (mot Z) consisted of a staff company (to KStN 1106) and three s PzJgKp (to KStN 1146) equipped with 36 guns, 12 in each company.

An 8.8cm PaK 43, mounted on a cruciform-type carriage, has been positioned on a hill so that its effective range of over 2,500m can be used to full advantage. But by being static they could be targeted by enemy artillery or fired on by ground-attack aircraft.

Due to being difficult to move, the 8.8cm PaK would be positioned in groups of three so that fire could be concentrated on a mass attack by Soviet tanks as it developed. The considerable effective range of the gun allowed it to be sited some distance behind the frontline.

A total of 18 independent H PzJgAbt were established.

Combined Artillery Battalions

In June 1943, the OKH decided to reorganize the light artillery battalions of the 11 infantry divisions – 15, 26, 68, 82, 88, 167, 294, 332, 333, 335 and 387 – in *Heeresgruppe Mitte* and *Heeresgruppe Süd* as *gemischte Artillerie-Abteilungen* (gem ArtAbt – combined artillery battalions). These battalions consisted of two batteries of four 10.5cm le FH 18 (horse drawn) and one battery having three 8.8cm PaK 43/41 (t mot, partially motorized). The PaK 43/41 battery was organized according KStN 433a with alterations. Mobility of the three guns was 'ensured' by one SdKfz 6 and three *Maultier* (mule) half-track trucks (type unknown).

Thus the concerned units would have received twelve 8.8cm PaK 43/41, a significant reinforcement for these infantry divisions. It is not known whether more units were modified like this. On the contrary, a request to issue 8.8cm

PaK 43 platoons to the *Panzergrenadier* divisions was rejected by October 1943, because there was a shortage of guns. Prime target was to provide guns to the s HPzJgAbt, which were still 120 weapons short.

Army Artillery Anti-tank Battalions

In May 1944, the OKH ordered the establishment of *Heeres Artillerie-Panzerabwehrkanone-Abteilungen* (H ArtPaKAbt – army artillery anti-tank gun battalions) and for all to be equipped with 7.5cm PaK 40 and/or 8.8cm PaK 43. But due to the ever-present shortage of replacement or new equipment, they were organized as *bodenständig* (bo) indicating they were equipped with captured, often obsolete, prime movers. Unlike those anti-tank units that were part of the *Panzertruppe*, these units belonged to the artillery. The H ArtPaKAbt (bo) was formed of a reduced staff company (to KStN 413) and three combat batteries (to KStN 460), each equipped with nine 8.8cm PaK 43 guns. All the units, like many others, lacked sufficient transport: The staff company had four passenger vehicles and two motorcycles; each battery had a passenger vehicle and a motorcycle. The supply column was issued two – one carrying a field kitchen – trucks and a further six trucks for transporting ammunition. The guns would be moved by a *Transportstaffel* (transport squadron). All units equipped with

Winter 1943: The crew of this 8.8cm PaK 43/41 has carefully positioned the gun behind a bank of earth, in preparation for an expected Russian counterattack. The commander is using an *Entfernungsmesser* (rangefinder) 36 to determine the exact range to the target.

All pioneer battalions were ordered to deliver their SdKfz 6 half-track tractors to units equipped with 8.8cm PaK 43/41. Many of these vehicles had been in service for many years and consequently were in poor mechanical condition.

8.8cm PaK 43 were supplied with nine SdKfz 7 half-tracks, and nine tractors for 27 guns. However, according to the war diary of the *General der Artillerie*, a number of Italian-built FIAT Spa TM 40 tractors were supplied to several units, but the type was not popular since it had no space for ammunition. Those units equipped with the PaK 40 were supplied with 15 *Rauppenschlepper-Ost* (RSO – fully-tracked tractor: East).

Communication on the battlefront was mostly by field telephone, but the lines were often destroyed by enemy fire. A few portable transceivers had been delivered, but no other radio equipment had been supplied,

The units were not only deployed in the anti-tank role but also as long-range artillery. But although having formidable firepower, to be an effective mobile force all units were reliant on the half-track or fully-tracked tractor for hauling the guns cross-country in all terrain conditions.

In June 1944, four ArtPaKAbt – 1007, 1008, 1009 and 1010 – were established and equipped with the 8.8cm PaK 43. Another 14 battalions – 1053 to 1066 – were equipped with the 7.5cm PaK 40.

Mobility

In 1943, the bombing of German heavy industries intensified when the USAAF began operations and the Ruhr was subjected to day and night raids. Subsequently production of weapons all other military equipment was severely affected, including the supply of a suitable tractor to tow the new heavy anti-tank gun. The 8.8cm PaK 43/41 weighed some 4,500kg, but the later 8.8cm PaK 43 was considerably heavier at 5,400kg and it became imperative for the problem to be solved before the type went into production.

Although military authorities were aware that mounting a heavy anti-tank gun on an armoured tracked chassis had many advantages and this was, in general, accepted by front-line officers, there were those who saw the lower profile of the towed anti-tank gun as more advantageous.

German vehicle manufacturers in the years before the war had designed and developed a number of half-tracked tractors with different hauling capacities – SdKfz 6, Sdkfz 7, SdKfz 8, SdKfz 9, SdKfz 10 and SdKfz 11. But, although the machines were very effective, they were time-consuming and expensive to build: production could never match with demand, resulting in a constant shortage. Further problems arose when in service; workshop crews found the halftracks difficult to maintain due to the complexity of transmission.

For this reason, a simplified half-tracked tractor, *schwerer Wehrmacht-sschlepper* (SWS – heavy military tractor) was ordered in late 1942 and was intended to replace both the SdKfz 6 and SdKfz 7 in production: But these plans would never be fully realized. Initially it was planned to use the SWS as a tractor for towing the 8.8cm PaK 43, but supplying sufficient vehicles would, as always, be problematic. Production of the type commenced in spring 1943, with a planned monthly output of 150 units, but the first vehicles were not delivered until that December. It has been suggested that approximately 820 had been completed by May 1945.

But in January 1943, an order was issued for the urgent development of a new type of heavy *Maultier*. A somewhat strange and baffling decision, since the *Maultier* concept was nothing more than a truck fitted with a half-track assembly and had a questionable towing performance. In an attempt to make up for the lack of SWS, Daimler-Benz fitted their Mercedes L 4500

The 8.8cm PaK 43/1 L/71 auf *Geschützwagen* III/IV was identified in the German ordnance inventory as the *Sonderkraftfahrzeug* (Sdkfz - special purpose vehicle) 164. This was not changed when the type was renamed *Nashorn* (rhinoceros). The troops are from a *Luftwaffe* field unit.

truck chassis (capacity 4.5t) with the running gear from a PzKpfw II Ausf C. Designated SdKfz 3/5 some 1,480 had been built by the end of the war.

The need for more tractors for 8.8cm PaK 43-equipped units became so desperate that military planners issued orders for large numbers of half-track vehicles (SdKfz 6 and Sdkfz 7) to be commandeered from pioneer units, leaving them to use wheeled trucks.

Organizational structure KStN 1146, published in June 1944, shows that the SdKfz 7 was only vehicle authorized to tow 8.8cm PaK 43/41 and 43.

A New Self-propelled Gun

Officials working at the *Waffenamt* were fully aware that all the types of motor vehicle available were unsuitable for towing the new heavy anti-tank gun and immediately demanded the development of a self-propelled version mounting the 8.8cm PaK.

A damaged SdKfz 164 from s PzJgAbt 519: Engineers have removed the drive sprocket and the final-drive unit; a complex item which could only be repaired at a field workshop.

A first suggestion was to utilize the chassis being designed for the projected le FH 43 self-propelled gun; another proposal was to adapt the PzKpfw II chassis as used on for the *Geschützwagen* (GW – gun carrier) II. Neither progressed any further. However, it is interesting to note that those same officials were giving some consideration to a proposal for mounting a 7.5cm PaK 44 on a GW II chassis.

To solve their dilemma an interim solution was required and they contracted Altmärkische Kettenwerke (Alkett), a company with wide experience in the manufacture of armoured and tracked vehicles) to design, develop and build a self-propelled gun using components from the PzKpfw III and PzKpfw IV.

Designated GW III/IV, the type originally mounted a 15cm s FH 18 field howitzer, or an 8.8cm PaK 43/1 anti-tank gun.

On 2 October 1942, pre-production models of both types of GW III/IV were shown at a weapons demonstration. Hitler was impressed and ordered the type into production while demanding that 100 of each type were to be delivered by 12 May 1943.

The commander of an SdKfz 164 *Nashorn* receives a message from a horse-mounted soldier, possibly from an infantry or *Volksgrenadier* division since both units would have been issued with a large number of horses. The standard 40cm tracks have been fitted with ice cleats to improve grip in mud and snow.

The self-propelled gun was designated *schwerer Panzerjäger auf Geschützwagen* III/IV *Hornisse*. This name would later be changed to *Nashorn* by *Führerbefehl*.

Organization

According to documents produced by the OrgAbt, it was planned to issue the first *Hornisse*, as they were delivered, to anti-tank battalions in selected Panzer divisions for fighting enemy tanks at long range.

The planned allocation was quickly altered: instead of being deployed in company strength they were to be organized in battalions at army group level, in a similar fashion to towed 8.8cm PaK 43/41 units. Originally distributed according KStN 1148b, dated January 1943, each company was authorized to receive ten *Hornisse*. A revised structure produced in April, authorized this to be increased to 14 in each company.

At the beginning of April 1943, the following units were established with three companies each:

- s PzJgAbt 560
- s PzJgAbt 655
- s PzJgAbt 525
- s PzJgAbt 519
- s PzJgAbt 93
- s PzJgAbt 88

Two further units were issued with smaller numbers of the type:

- s PzJgAbt 664
- PzJgKp 660

In December 1944, only PzJgAbt 93 and 88 were still issued with *Panzerjäger Nashorn* (tank destroyer rhinoceros).

In July 1943, the s HPzJgAbt 661 (formerly HPzJgAbt 'A') submitted an extensive report on the first experiences with the PaK 43/41 (motor traction):

s HPzJgAbt 661 ('A')
Tactical and technical experiences with the s PaK 43/41 (8.8cm) for the period from 17 July to 30 July 1943

1. Leadership

a)

Good communications are indispensable for leading the company. Due to the wide area of deployment the company commander is at present unable to lead his company as effectively as he wished. The battalion staff must be provided with long-range (5W) radio equipment.

b)

Only a well-trained, capable and energetic platoon leader is suitable to command this heavy weapon. This applies also to the company and battalion leader.

c)

It is advisable to establish a PaK liaison officer for the infantry in the front-line positions. This officer is responsible for immediately reporting to the PaK platoon when any of our infantry begin to withdraw. Close cooperation with the infantry is of utmost importance.

d)

A large-scale enemy tank assault can quickly lead to all ammunition being expended. A most strict organization of the supply within the battalion, company and platoon is absolutely vital. The prevailing weather conditions on the Mius Front, has meant that only fast and agile tracked vehicles can be used to re-supply our positions.

An Sdkfz 164 from the s PzJgAbt 519 has been attached to a sledge-mounted heated accommodation unit, which would provide some comfort in the harsh winter conditions of the Eastern Front.

The *Hornisse* gunner relied on a *Selbstfahrlafette-Zielfernrohr* (Sfl ZF – [self-propelled] gunsight) 1a, a *Beobachtungsfernrohr* (BF – observation periscope) for direct and indirect fire. Early versions were issued with a direct *Zielfernrohr* (ZF – vision telescope) and a *Zieleinrichtung* (panoramic sight) 34.

e)

Any enemy tank which had broken through our lines was actively pursued. A gun was ordered to leave its front-line position and attached to the front of a halftrack. The combination carefully stalked the tank before opening fire and destroying the intruder. Despite being supported by enemy infantry any tank which had broken through was neutralized in this way.

2. Gun position

The guns were positioned, without exception, as conditions on the battlefield developed. In most instances any form of reconnaissance was impossible.

a)

To give our infantry the necessary support we were often forced to fire down on the enemy from a sloping position. This proved better than expected, since the guns could not be spotted behind the slope. The tractors were withdrawn to safety, but were kept close-by and ready to move.

b)

The gunners should not fire on a target at a range of over 2,400m since accuracy is reduced and ammunition is wasted.

c)

Whenever possible, the guns must operate in unison so that an enemy tank can be attacked in a 'pincer' of fire.

Two SdKfz 164 *Nashorn* from s PzJgAbt 88 positioned on high ground overlooking the flat landscape near the city of Orjol. The badge of the unit was a sword over an oak, which would be stencilled on a front track guard.

German pioneers have utilized a *Brückengerät* 'B' bridging section by positioning it on four pontoon boats to create a ferry; here carrying an SdKfz 164. Pioneer units had at their disposal components to build bridges with load capacities ranging from 4,060kg to 20,320kg. These items could also be used to assemble a *Sonderfähre* (special ferry) 52 to transport up to 60,960kg.

d)

When a gun is moved to new position the crew must dig rifle pits [trenches] immediately. The situation on the battlefront never allowed sufficient time for the construction of an earth wall to protect the gun.

e)

Alternative firing positions must be pre-prepared ready to move into to if attacked enemy artillery; this proved to be more dangerous than tank fire. The battalion lost five guns to enemy artillery, but only one to tank fire.

f)

Most dangerous was when massed enemy artillery targeted our gun positions. In one case, after the enemy had laid smoke making observation of the battlefront impossible, our positions were overrun by 30 to 40 tanks. We were able to destroy just six T-34s, but five guns and their tractors had to be abandoned. Although all were recovered later, such a situation must be avoided. Some guns must be placed to establish provide defensive cover on the flanks of our positions.

3. Training

a)

The s PaK 43/41 must be operated by only the best-trained *Panzerjäger* gunners. Those operating with the s PaK 43/41 must not only be physically fit, but also mentally alert. The half-track driver must be tactically aware and experienced to be able to effectively assist the gun crew during a battle.

b)

The s PaK 43/41 is a very heavy weapon and will always require a full crew: commander and eight *mannschaften* [enlisted men]. Otherwise, it would be impossible to traverse or limber the gun. Traversing the gun on wet ground was extremely difficult, even by a full crew. A strong reserve crew is essential.

4. The weapon

a)

In one instance, the spent cartridge was not ejected. After every round fired, the crew was forced to push the cartridge out using the cleaning rod. A careful examination of the cartridges was inconclusive, but the jams only occurred when firing PzGr 39 ammunition.

A *Nashorn* of 1./s PzJgAbt 88. To identify the companies in each battalion, the suits from playing cards were used: Staff company Diamonds; 1.Kp. Clubs; 2.Kp Spades and 3.Kp Hearts.

Heavy *Panzerjäger Nashorn* [*Hornisse*] SdKfz 164

Weapon	8.8cm PaK 43/1 (see above)
Secondary armament	One MG 34, two MP 40
Height of muzzle	2,260mm
Traverse	30 degrees
Elevation range	-5 degrees to +20 degrees
Weight	24,000kg
Engine	Maybach HL 120 TRM
Power	265hp
Speed (maximum)	40kph
Range (road)	260km
Range (off road)	130km
Ammunition storage	40 HE and AP rounds
Communication	FuSprGer 'f' transceiver, intercom Command vehicle Fu 8

b)
After changing firing position three times, a few of our guns had become
seriously misaligned and had to be withdrawn from the battlefront.
c)
Scattering at ranges up to 2,000m was noted as being average.
d)...
e)
Gunner No.3 has to be issued with a sufficient number of cleaning cloths.
To avoid jams the rounds must be thoroughly cleaned before being passed to
the loader.
f)...
g)
After a firefight, the gun can become bogged down on soft ground and be
impossible for the crew to move. In this situation a gun tractor will be required,
but the tow hook on the vehicle must be very carefully aligned with the eye
on the carriage.

5. Ammunition
The ammunition was supplied in equal proportions, but this did not prove to
be effective. Suggestion: 75 per cent AP rounds and 25 per cent HE rounds.

6. Final assessment
Despite our relatively high loss of personnel, weaponry and tractors – three
PaK and five halftracks – our troops consider the s PaK as the best and also

Above: An 8.8cm PaK 43/41 in combat: The K1 (gunner) has stepped away from the breech to avoid the recoil; three of the crew wait in line with ammunition ready to pass to K2 (loader) to place in the breech when ordered by the gun commander.

Left: According regulations, an 8.8cm PaK 43/41 was to have a crew of nine: the commander, a gunner, a loader and six men. This was strictly adhered to in order to move the heavy gun in an emergency.

In January 1943, a wooden mock-up of the Krupp-built 8.8cm PaK 43, with a cruciform-type carriage mounted on a trailer, was presented to Hitler at a demonstration of new and proposed weapons. Suitably impressed, he demanded that it should be put into production immediately, but this proved to be impossible. Instead, mass production of the 8.8cm PaK 43/41 towed anti-tank gun was begun in February 1943.

most reliable weapon. After six days in combat we had destroyed 127 enemy tanks (T-34, KV-1 and one General Lee).

It has been noted, in a number of after-action reports, that the SdKfz 6 was too light and underpowered to be an effective gun tractor for the 8.8cm PaK 43/41. Consequently, the majority of units were supplied with only the SdKfz 7; at least that was the plan. Once again, due to the lack of materials and German heavy industry being decimated by Allied bombing raids, delivery of these valuable tractors almost stopped. Front-line forces had to be content with whatever vehicles were available.

The s H PzJgAbt 662 (formlery s H PzJgAbt 'B'), deployed with *Heeresgruppe Süd*, submitted an after-action report in August 1943. Interestingly, it was published in the *Nachrichtenblatt der Panzertruppen* (bulletin of the armoured troops) and included comments made by the *Generalinspekteur der Panzertruppen*:

Experiences with 8.8cm PaK 43/41 mot Z

1.)

During defensive battles, the mobility of the 8.8cm PaK 43/41 proved to be better than expected. During a rapid change of positions an average speed of 25kph was achieved (the urgent transfer of 1.Kp from Solotarevka to Sslavjansk took only 2 hours). Any such emergency movement will always require the personnel involved to receive a thorough briefing. When moving to new positions, the supply of ammunition must be delivered without any delay. Repeatedly, we were forced to change position while being observed and subsequently attacked enemy artillery. On some occasions we were strafed by enemy aircraft. A commander must do everything possible to avoid changing firing position under such conditions, since it could result in the loss of an entire platoon.

Although the 8.8cm PaK 43/41 was an excellent weapon, the Krupp solution was far superior; their 8.8cm PaK 43 could be fired directly from the carriage, allowing the gun to be traversed through 360 degrees, and was operated by a smaller crew.

The towed 8.8cm PaK 43/41 was 20cm higher than a 8.8cm PaK 43 proposed by Krupp and shown to Hitler in January 1943.

Comment of the GenInsp d PzTrp:

Despite lacking mobility, the 8.8cm PaK has been assessed as favourable, and it must be remembered that any rapid [emergency] transfers will be the absolute exception. Instead a pre-planned deployment at focal points must be aimed for, using thoroughly reconnoitred and well-prepared firing positions (refer to the instruction pamphlet). Furthermore, a PaK-*Kampftrupp* [combat squad]. should be formed to operate in close cooperation with other light, medium and heavy anti-tank guns.

2.)
The majority of the enemy tanks we destroyed were not engaged from well-prepared locations, but from random positions. Thanks to being very mobile, the 8.8cm PaK 43/41 units were able to move to previously selected positions in hedgerows, villages, woodland and even a field of growing corn. But it is essential that any position can easily and rapidly be vacated after a defensive action. If the situation makes it impossible for the guns to be moved, then they will have to dug-in for added protection. But this action should be the exception, and only carried out if the guns are threatened.

3.)
The accuracy of the guns proved to be extraordinarily high; in some cases tanks were shot down at ranges over 3,000m. To maintain accuracy, all guns must be realigned after a march [transfer].

Comment of the GenInsp d PzTrp:
The most effective firing range of the 8.8cm PaK is less than 2,000m. Any long-range fire at enemy tanks should only happen in an exceptional circumstance; when defending against any enemy tank formation which has begun a direct attack on our gun positions. Forward observers are essential, and selective expenditure of ammunition will help to achieve success.

4.)
All s PzJgAbt equipped with the 8.8cm PaK 43 must not be deployed for long periods in one position near the *Hauptkampflinie* (HKL – main line of resistance). To make best use of this accurate long-range weapon they should be moved to positions defending focal points.

The remarks inserted by the GenInsp d PzTrp indicate that he had some previous experience and was thoroughly aware of the situation. His insistence on conserving ammunition seems fine in practice, but in the heat of battle the

	100mm BS-3	8.8cm PaK 43	12.8cm PaK 80
Calibre	10cm	8.8cm	12.8cm
Weight (travelling mode)	3,460kg	5,400kg	10,160kg
Barrel length	5m	6.25m	7.04m
V°	900mps	1,000mps	920mps
Armour penetration 1,500m	20cm	14.8cm	19cm

Two *Nashorn* self-propelled guns from 1./s PzJgAbt 88 positioned to allow maximum side traverse. The vehicle to the left is being supplied with ammunition from a 3-ton truck.

troops would fire any number of rounds at any enemy tank until it retreated or immobilized.

As the battle continued, Soviet forces found a way to neutralize the threat of German long-range anti-tank guns. Before launching an attack by tanks and supporting infantry, their massed artillery would open fire and bombard German lines, particularly anti-tank gun positions. Frequently, the Soviet air force would be called to follow the barrage with a number of air strikes.

In February 1944, H PzJgAbt 664 submitted an after-action report:

A report on the commitment of the 8.8cm PaK 43/41 (mot Z)

The following observations were made during the deployment of the battalion in the defensive battles around Vitebsk, between 1 November 1943 and 10 February 1944.

The claim that the 8.8cm PaK 43/41 can destroy enemy tanks attacking ahead of our HKL can only be achieved under very specific conditions, but these will not always prevail in the majority of cases. In an ideal situation, the HKL has

Far left: The drive sprocket and *Seitenvorgelage* (final-drive assembly) used on the *Geschützwagen* (GW – gun carrier) III/IV was taken from a PzKpfw III Ausf F, but slightly widened to allow the fitment of 40cm tracks. Note the lashing eyes, which have been fitted to the sides of the superstructure by field engineers.

to be situated behind a slope; a rare occurrence. Normally the infantry would prefer to set the HKL on the front edge of a slope. But this would restrict our anti-tank guns.

During recent fighting, the enemy tended to initiate every attack with a massive artillery barrage, which ranged across 2km to 3km of the territory we held. In most instances the enemy opened the attack with an infantry assault, carefully holding his tanks beyond the maximum range of our anti-tank weapons. The artillery barrage did not destroy or damage any of our PaK, but the crews were forced to fire at the attacking infantry. During these skirmishes, a number of gun positions were overrun and neutralized, and the subsequent loss of personnel and equipment was considerable. Since all of our half-track tractors had been put out of action, it was impossible to reposition any of our guns.

Thus, for any static commitment of 8.8cm PaK to effectively defend our front-line troops, the guns must be sited in well-camouflaged and thoroughly prepared fortified positions some distance to the rear.

However, under direct command of higher levels [army], the 8.8cm PaK is the most effective weapon for defeating any enemy tank that has penetrated our lines. During the recent fighting east of Vitebsk, the battalion successfully accomplish its mission of halting any breakthroughs by enemy tanks. Their success was due, in part, to the absence of a pre-assault bombardment by enemy artillery. This allowed our guns to be sited in open firing positions; these were later fortified. But the Russians, without warning, began an artillery barrage and our positions became untenable; the guns were rapidly moved to the rear.

A company of s H PzJgAbt 560 was issued with ten – one command and eight combat – SdKfz 164 in accordance with KStN 1148b, dated 30 January 1943. The document makes no reference to the issue of a Steyr 1500 command car, three VW *Typ* 82 *Kübelwagen* (bucket-seat car).

The 8.8cm PaK 43/1 gun on this SdKfz 164 of s H PzJgAbt 655, is at maximum elevation and a *Maschinengewehr* (MG – machine gun) 34 has been mounted for air defence.

After evaluating these experiences, the battalion is of the opinion that the 8.8cm PaK (mot Z) should be replaced by a sufficient number of *Hornisse* self-propelled guns.

On 22 January 1944, this experience report was submitted to AOK 3 and then forwarded to the *Generalinspekteur der Panzertruppen*:

Experience report on the commitment of 8.8 cm Pak 43 (mot Z) in *Großkämpfen* (great battles)

The above-mentioned commitment took place in accordance with Pamphlet 18/9, dated 27 June 1943.

The army had previously issued, on 28 December 1943, an order which forbade the 8.8cm PaK 43/41 being placed under the command of a battalion, and was issued after evaluating experience reports submitted following recent fighting. Significantly, it effectively indentifies the disadvantageous ratio of victories to losses suffered by towed 8.8cm PaK units.

The order was originally issued after an examination had been made of the experience report submitted by PzJgAbt 664. The *Panzerarmee* had previously published an instructional pamphlet which referred to an increase in combat operations by Russian tank units, but we did note they showed some caution, possibly to reduce their losses. The heavy preparatory artillery barrage allowed their infantry to break through our lines and they were followed by a large force of tanks.

In order to neutralize the feared 8.8cm PaK, Soviet infantry changed their tactics and began to seek out guns and then attack, but many would have been destroyed by the preliminary artillery barrage. Although this proved to be an effective means of reducing tank losses it came at a price: their infantry suffered appalling losses, but Red Army commanders saw the tank as being a more valuable battlefield asset than a simple infantryman. Also, they were comfortable with the knowledge of the vast, almost endless, numbers of infantry personnel held in reserve and the numbers being conscripted.

When commanders at Pz AOK 3 compared the experiences of s HPzJgAbt 664 (towed 8.8cm PaK) and s PzJgAbt 519 (*Hornisse*), they discovered that both battalions were equally well supplied with equipment and acknowledged that their leadership was experienced, energetic and effective. Also, they noted that both units had seen action in almost identical circumstances.

From September 1943 to 10 February 1944, s H PzJgAbt 664 managed to destroy a total of 88 enemy tanks, but lost 18 8.8cm PaK (mot Z), 12 SdKfz 6, one heavy *Maultier*, two 2-ton *Maultier* and also four RSO. The unit also suffered a number of casualties; 30 killed, 160 wounded and 21 listed as missing in action.

The *Hornisse*-equipped s PzJgAbt 519 was much more effective. In the period 20 December 1943 to 10 February 1944, the unit destroyed 290 enemy tanks, but lost six *Hornisse*. However, due to a lack of SdKfz 9 recovery tractors, four of the six self-propelled guns had to be blown up by the crews. If these vehicles had been available, all would have been recovered and repaired.

In the further course of their assessment, Pz AOK 3 issued a straightforward questionnaire:

Are the guidelines given in Pamphlet 18/9, regarding combat use of the 8.8cm PaK (mot Z), ineffective in the light of combat experience?

Answer: Yes

The recovery of a damaged or mechanically-failed vehicle was vitally important and crews were encouraged to be prepared. Here the crew of an SdKfz 164 has fitted shackles to the towing eyes and prepared the recovery hawser.

Is there any sense in continuing to produce the towed 8.8cm PaK?

Answer: No

Will the introduction of the *Kreuzlafette* (cruciform carriage) solve these problems?

Answer: No

Is there a better solution?

Answer: Increase production of *Hornisse*

Commitment

In February 1944, Major Hoppe, commander of s PzJgAbt 519, submitted an after-action report:

Experience report from s PzJgAbt 519

Tactical experiences

The rolling terrain, but free of obstacles, provided ideal conditions for attacking small formations of enemy tanks. However, after few kilometres the enemy was forced to enter a narrow bottleneck. Subsequently, our battalion massed all available anti-tank weapons ready to attack.
As usual, the infantry demanded that our heavy anti-tank weapons be deployed in close proximity to the HKL; they even suggested that should include the

On early versions of the SdKfz 164 the exhaust silencer [muffler] was mounted on the rear plate. But this was soon removed from production vehicles due to the fumes from the exhaust entering the fighting compartment.

Hornisse. The staff echelon of the *Panzerarmee* clarified the situation and issued a strict order covering the tactical deployment of the type.

The true combat value of the *Hornisse* is in its mobility and long-range gun.

Many infantry commanders tended to order the *Hornisse* into action as a tank without consulting the *Panzerjäger*, which invariably led to the loss of a valuable combat asset. Subsequently, an order was issued to the commanders of all *Hornisse* battalions encouraging them to question any deployment with the infantry. But, all too often he had to seek for backing from a more senior officer.

During the commitment of s H PzJgAbt 519, the army issued clear instructions:

Any deployment will be made only on orders from the [*Hornisse*] company leader after evaluating the mission and completing a thorough reconnaissance of the terrain. It is his responsibility to determine the location of suitable firing positions and assembly areas. Also, he must have selected alternative sites and fully briefed his *Hornisse* crews.

The deployment of a sole *Hornisse*, in *wilde Jagd* ['wild hunting'] style to stalk the enemy, has proven to be highly effective, but the vehicle must be commanded by an experienced officer or NCO.

The vehicle must never be deployed as a tank: the battalion recently lost two *Hornisse* due to orders being ignored. The Red Army has begun to insert anti-tank teams within the spearhead of an attack.

Commitment of the Russian tank force

Before launching a major attack, the Russian will have completed a very thorough reconnaissance to identify any weak points in our defensive positions. The Russian avoids massed tank assaults, but now opens an attack with a heavy artillery bombardment with the intention of demoralizing or destroying our infantry and also eliminating our anti-tank defences. The shelling is followed by an attack by massed infantry.

Deployment

The deployment of the vehicle should take place only in company strength within a sector occupied by a division. When a focal point was created, we always deployed two companies accompanied by the battalion staff.

When attached to a division we have noticed that our *Hornisse* commanders were

Far left: The unit badge s PzJgAbt 655 has been painted on the right-hand track guard; on the left is stencilled the tactical sign for a self-propelled anti-tank gun. In August 1944, the staff company of s PzJgAbt 655, accompanied by 1.Kp and 2.Kp, was transferred to Mielau (Mława) in Poland to be equipped with the SdKfz 173 *Jagdpanther* (hunting panther). The 3.Kp, equipped with 14 *Nashorn*, remained in the Soviet Union.

never given general missions to protect the divisional sector. Instead a single gun would be ordered into a randomly selected static position, negating the full value of the type's mobility and firepower. The guns must never be massed together, since they would become a target for enemy artillery and mortar batteries.

Many front-line commanders suffering from 'tank nervousness' ordered the *Hornisse* into position before an attack had developed and sometimes before any enemy tanks had been spotted. Difficult terrain conditions often meant that the self-propelled guns were inactive for long periods. With the guns held in front-line defensive positions for long periods, thorough routine maintenance was impossible.

On many occasions where a commander, after conducting a reconnaissance, offered his opinion or suggestion it would seldomly be accepted, particularly if it differed from that of a senior officer.

Now that the Russian deploys his tank forces differently for an attack, our *Hornisse* must never be used as an emplaced gun, since any rapid or urgent movement to a focal point of an attack will be impossible. Instead, immediately after a mission has been completed, they must return to their collection point to be prepared for the next combat operation.

A massed deployment of all available *Hornisse* is wrong and is strictly forbidden. At least one platoon must be held in reserve by the company commander. For instance, a force of some eight *Hornisse* were requested to repel an assault by between 10 or 15 enemy tanks where four self-propelled guns would have been more than sufficient to achieve success.

Example: On one occasion a platoon of three *Hornisse* destroyed 22 out of 47 attacking tanks within 27 minutes. One alone destroyed 14, the second six and the third two tanks.

Before any *Hornisse* are committed a thorough reconnaissance of the surrounding terrain must be completed. Quite often the most favourable positions will be found outside our own regimental or divisional sectors. Two *Hornisse* were positioned in adjacent divisional sectors to provide defensive flanking fire. Not only was this successful, but it also kept them hidden from enemy tanks and out of range for his artillery.

It is very important for the guns to frequently change position, since this will make it more difficult for the enemy to locate and attack our *Hornisse*. Also, it should help to disguise our focal points of defence.

There is an overall lack of consistent command for the anti-tank defences within the divisional sectors. Heavy anti-tank guns were sited in emplacements and used for short-range defence, whereas medium anti-tank guns were positioned to fire at long-range targets.

On many occasions, units equipped with the Tiger, *Hornisse* and *Sturmgeschütz* were available to defend focal points, but the commanders were never called to a joint briefing to discuss defensive tactics. Many units were not aware of where others were positioned; on a number of occasions being hit by supporting or friendly fire was only avoided at the very last moment. The period around dawn or at dusk was the most the dangerous.

All anti-tank defences must be combined under the control of a highly experienced *Panzerjäger-Kommandeur* (anti-tank defence commander),

A damaged SdKfz 164, from an unknown battalion, attached to an SdKfz 9 for recovery to a field workshop. Note, the vehicle has the latest type of *Ostketten* (east tracks) normally used in winter conditions.

An 8.8cm PaK 43 has been carefully positioned and is almost hidden from an enemy observer. But after firing a few rounds (revealing its position) the gun would have to be moved to avoid a counterstrike by enemy artillery.

who must be able to integrate the *Panzerjäger* with the available tanks and *Sturmgeschütz* and constantly liaise with the leaders of the units.

The radio communication must be improved, the diversity of radio equipment supplied causes many problems. For instance, many an astute unit leader has overcome this by linking different radio posts. Importantly, radio messages must be carefully authenticated to avoid any misunderstandings. In one case, an attack by 84 tanks was reported, but after anti-tank forces had been mobilized it was found that the 'offensive' was being made by only four to eight tanks.

The commander must be free of any interference from divisional or regimental staff, since they are front-line forces and should lead from their command tanks or from effective observation posts.

The 8.8cm PaK 43 was certainly a most effective anti-tank weapon and gave the *Panzerjäger* a clear advantage when fighting enemy armour until the end of World War II. However, as evidenced in many after-action reports, the towed anti-tank weapon was only effective when a sufficient number of suitable tractor vehicles were available. The solution was an effective self-propelled gun; the *Hornisse* which mounted a powerful 8.8cm PaK on a purpose-built chassis for efficient mobility.

However, the Russians were also introducing more powerful weapons. In March 1945, the *Gruppe Ausbildung* (instructional group) at the *Generalinspekteur der Panzertruppe* delivered a memorandum:

New heavy Russian 10cm L/58 anti-tank gun

To effectively defeat our heavy tanks and *Jagdpanzer*, the Russian has developed a heavy anti-tank gun which has been encountered recently. Russian designation: 100mm gun 44 BS-3.

A comparison is interesting: The gun barrel was fitted with a double-baffle muzzle brake and mounted on a split-trail carriage, with torsion bar suspension, carried on two double wheels with pneumatic rubber tyres. Originally the gun, which had a very low profile, was issued to towed anti-tank gun units. The gun was also mounted in the SU-100 tank destroyer.

Total enemy air superiority over the battlefield, meant that camouflage was essential for survival. This was important for the crew of a *Nashorn/Hornisse* since their vehicle was very large with a distinctive profile it would be essential for them to find suitable cover. A farm with outbuildings and stacks of hay was considered to be ideal.

Front-line Weapons 5

During 1943, increasing numbers of more effective anti-tank guns were being delivered to *Panzerjäger* units in infantry divisions, tank divisions, and also army troop formations. These included a number mounted as self-propelled guns to provide the German army with significantly more mobility on the battlefront and help ease the dire situation faced by troops under attack by massed formations of Soviet tanks.

The introduction of the towed 8.8cm PaK 43 and especially the similarly armed *Hornisse* self-propelled gun represented a quantum leap. For the first time since the launch of *Unternehmen* Barbarossa, German front-line forces now had superior weapons available that were capable of defeating Russian armour.

The 8.8cm KwK L/71 was introduced by the *Waffenamt* not only to modernize existing armoured vehicles, but also for mounting in new and more effective types being developed for future service.

In the summer of 1943, the *Samokhodnya Ustanovka* (SU – self-propelled installation) 152 *Zveroboy* (tank slayer) intended to fight the PzKpfw VI Tiger tank was seen on the battlefield; as was the KV-85, an upgraded version of the KV-1S and the first Russian tank to mount an 85mm gun. However, neither type troubled German anti-tank units now they were receiving more powerful and effective weapons.

Military planners were faced with another problem; the Red Army not only had better armoured tanks, but had also altered its combat tactics. German front-line troops in trenches were often overrun and had to fight tanks with hand grenades; an effective close-quarters anti-tank weapon was urgently required.

A soldier from the *Gebirgsjäger* (mountain infantry) armed with a *Panzerfaust* (tank fist) 30. Stitched on his sleeve are three *Panzerkampfabzeichen* (tank combat badges). On his tunic there is an infantry assault badge and an *Eisernes Kreuz* (EK – Iron Cross) 2nd class.

The use of the *Hafthohlladung* (adhesive charge) 3kg required great courage; an infantryman had to wait in his trench ready to leap out and plant the charge on the tank. Used correctly, any tank could be destroyed.

One solution produced was a compact handheld and easily transportable weapon, with sufficient explosive power to defeat an enemy tank, which would be issued to front-line troops. The simple light-weight weapon was cheap and quick to manufacture which meant the type could (in theory) be issued to every individual infantryman. The weapon was also used to great effect where an anti-tank gun could not, particularly in an ambush situation.

This close-combat anti-tank weapon was soon accepted as a vital piece of equipment by the infantry; a concerted anti-tank defence force could be rapidly assembled. During numerous close-quarters battles, it was often found to be the only available anti-tank weapon. But the weapon could only be effective if sufficient numbers were available and the troops were correctly trained. However, using the weapon took outstanding courage by an individual soldier.

Continuing technical progress soon made many weapons, including the 7.92mm *Panzerbüchse* (PzB – tank hunting rifle) 39 which had been considered obsolete in 1940. The PzB 39 was effective against the Soviet T-26 or the BT series fought at the beginning of *Unternehmen* Barbarossa, whereas the Russian-built 14.5mm PTRS or PTRD anti-tank rifle was much more effective. Indeed, it was this weapon that caused the introduction of *Panzerschürzen* (side skirts): a large-scale operation that was initiated in the summer of 1943 to attach extra armour to most types of German tank and all assault guns.

The *Schießbecher* (projector), for fitting on the K98 carbine, was introduced in 1942 and was also available to mount on the shortened *Panzergranatbüchse* (PzGrB) 39. Both types proved to be effective, but only if conditions were favourable.

The most basic weapons (explosive charges, Molotov cocktails and mines) could be utilized with some chance of success, but usage was extremely hazardous and many infantrymen died as a result.

By early 1943, unlike the situation in 1941, German front-line infantry units had been supplied with a number of explosive devices powerful enough to immobilize or even destroy an enemy tank. One of the most effective weapons introduced was the 3kg *Hafthohlladung* (HaftHl – adhesive hollow charge). The weapon was fitted with three magnets to secure it on the armour plate and a special type of igniter so that detonation was delayed.

A *Feldwebel* Dräken, of 8./FeldErsBtl (7.PzDiv), submitted an after-action report in February 1943:

Close combat against tank using a 3kg HaftHl

While breaking through our lines at Donsas, south of Isjum, on 26 February 1943 a Soviet T-34 became stuck. Three of the crew abandoned the tank and attempted to escape. We proceeded with three men armed with *Hafthohlladung* [HaftHl], hand grenades and *Maschinenpistole* [MP – machine pistol] 44. When the remaining crew saw us, they threw hand grenades and then we were fired at by the *Maschinengewehr* [MG – machine gun] in the tank. Within a short time, the escaping crew were killed. While one of my men provided covering fire, we moved towards the tank just as the driver tried to escape. I jumped on the tank from behind and placed a HaftHl on the engine cover and after few seconds' delay, we heard a detonation that caused the engine to stop running. The second HaftHl was placed on the front of the turret where it detonated and penetrated the armour, killing the remaining crew.

To completely destroy the tank, we threw two hand grenades into the engine compartment: the detonation tore the tank to pieces.

An *Oberfeldwebel* (staff sergeant) at an anti-tank training establishment indicates where to place charges on a Soviet T-34. He wears four *Panzerkampfabzeichen* (tank combat badges) on his sleeve.
A *Hafthohlladung* 3kg and other other types of anti-tank explosive charge are on the table.

Conclusion:

Based on the experiences made during the eastern campaign, close combat against tanks has to be practised as often as possible by every unit. The HaftHl proved to be as the most effective close combat weapon.

The effectiveness of the weapon is confirmed in another after-action report submitted in 1944:

Oberjäger Neff, 14./MG Kp JägRgt 75

After successfully halting a Russian breakthrough near Dvorichtche on 3 January 1944, a Soviet T-34 came close to our positions. It stopped near to my foxhole and opened fire. I took my opportunity and ran to the tank, placing a HaftHl (yellow button type with seven seconds delay) on the side of the superstructure just below the turret ring. I instantly jumped back in my hole and then heard a detonation which set the tank on fire. After a few minutes, another loud internal detonation blew the turret off, which fell top down back on the chassis. While the tank continued to burn, I could see that the weapon had burnt a 2 to 3cm hole through the armour.

In August 1942, the *General der Schnellen Truppen* (GendSchnTrp – rapid troops) – when Guderian took command in February 1943 this department was renamed *General der Panzertruppen* (GendPzTrp – armoured troops) – issued an urgent demand for the development of a close-range anti-tank weapon:

The progressive design of different types of anti-tank weapon will lead to a decrease in the number of PaK guns available to front-line units, and this is not acceptable. [His remark suggests that the development and production of heavier weapons would consume whatever resources were available, resulting in fewer anti-tank guns being built.] We demand the immediate development of a *Panzernahschusswaffe* (close-range anti-tank weapon) for the infantry, and for it to be produced in substantial numbers to complement the available armour-piercing weapons.
Specification:

– Weight:
  15kg, at maximum 30kg to be transported in two loads (for better mobility in winter)

A Russian anti-tank team preparing to fire a captured late production (shortened barrel) *Rakketen-Panzerbüchse* (RaKPzB – rocket-assisted weapon) 54/1 at advancing German armour. (Getty)

– Penetration:

   90mm at 30 degrees

   120mm at 60 degrees

– Good accuracy at 150m to 200m range

– Easy to handle when fired from a prone position

The shortened PzGrB (*Panzergranatbüchse*) 39 matches parts of the above, but has poor armour penetration (70 to 80mm). Also, the weapon lacks accuracy and is difficult (even dangerous) to operate.

The GendSchnTrp considers the development of an effective close-range anti-tank weapon as being tactically vital to the infantry. To accelerate development, all other work must be postponed.

Despite his clear demands, some two months later the *Generalstab des Heeres* (GenStdH) again fervently requested the development of more powerful anti-tank weapons:

The early type *Panzerschreck* (tank fright) was delivered without a protective blast shield. Gunners were instructed to put on the protective hood, with integral air filter, and to wear heavy gloves, but this would be almost impossible in a combat situation. Front-line *Kampftruppe* (combat troops) made demands for the weapon to modified.

1.)

GenStdH demands the rapid development an anti-tank gun for the front-line infantry units, and suggests that it meets the following performance parameters:

Penetration:	150mm at 45 degrees sloped armour.
Weight:	250kg (maximum).
Firing height:	75cm approximately.
Combat range:	up to 400m.
Mobility:	Horse or motor towed, dismountable for transport on a vehicle, a pack animal or the crew.

2.)

An attachable grenade launcher is under development for the shortened PzB 39. The grenade fired from the K 98 rifle has a range 110m, but we expect the new *grosse Gewehr-Panzergranate* (gr GewPzGr – heavy rifle grenade device) to be effective at over 150m range.

Item1: The anti-tank gun specified by the GenStbdH seems to be the 8.8cm RaKWrf 43, but the proposed weight of 250kg would be far too high; even 50kg was considered too heavy for a soldier to carry and operate on the frontline.

Item 2: The PzB 39 firing the gr GewPzGr never reached the desired penetration data. Armour 70mm to 80mm thick was penetrated at maximum range. In a reply the commander expressed his vehement opposition.

In a further response the GenStdH finally agreed on these arguments provided that the armour penetration would be increased to 150mm to 200mm and the combat range to 200mm to 400m, considerably exceeding the initial claims of the GendSchnTrp.

However, the OKH published a short message by January 1944 emphasizing the good experiences made with the *Schießbecher* launcher. The ammunition supply was to be increased to 4,000,000 rounds AP and HE rounds per month.

Rocket-propelled ammunition: (top) 2.36-inch Bazooka M1; (centre) 8.8cm RaKPzB 54; (lower) *Panzerfaust* 60.

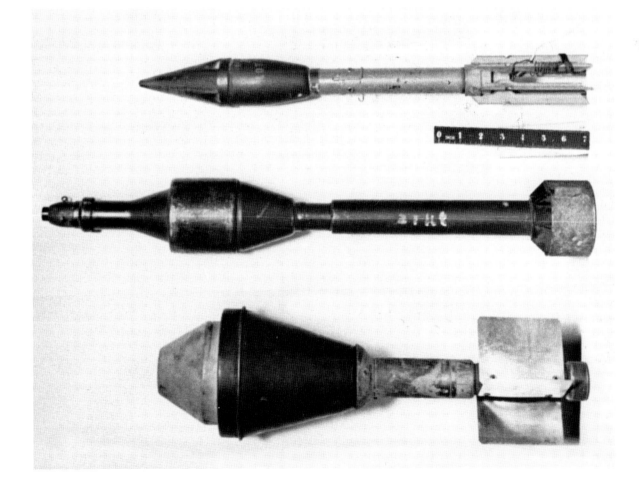

Far right: A German RaKPzB 54/1 (left) and a US Army Bazooka M1.

8.8cm *Raketen-Panzerbüchse* 54

The *Hohlladung* (HaftHl) had proven to be an excellent weapon for close combat against enemy tanks. The charge was easy to handle and despite using relatively simple technology it was very effective, but a soldier had to leave his position and get close, often under fire, to the tank to be able to place the device. The introduction into service of the short to medium range *Panzerschreck* and *Panzerfaust* would make life a little safer for the anti-tank infantry.

In 1943, German troops fighting in Tunisia captured an intact US Army M1 Bazooka, a man-portable recoilless anti-tank rocket launcher which fired a 2.36-inch projectile.

A short article on the weapon was published in the September 1943 issue of the *Bulletin der Panzertruppe*:

> The handbook captured together with the weapon gives the name Rocket Launcher anti-tank M1. The name 'Bazooka' is also used, but this might possibly be a code name. The weapon is extremely light, and is of simple construction. Essentially the weapon consists of a long tube, with two handles and a box attached. It can be operated in standing or prone position, but a two-man crew is necessary for rapid fire. On firing, the propellant jet is emitted straight from the rear. The gun sight attached on the left side is graduated at 90m, 180m, 270m and 360m, but the gunner has to estimate range, wind force and the speed of the target. The weapon weighs some 5kg. The rocket-propelled projectile has a shaped-charge warhead for maximum explosive effect and is stabilized by six simple fins attached to the rear. The propellant phase is contained by the projector tube and the flight to the target is purely ballistic. The projectile reaches a maximum speed of 90mps and the shaped-charge warhead shows no peculiarities. The rocket propellant is ignited electrically with power from a battery.
>
> We trialled the weapon and ammunition by firing on a 2m-square gun shield target at a range of 100m; the result, 20 rounds fired and 20 hits. Penetration of 80mm steel was achieved at an impact angle of 60 degrees. The trajectory of the projectile was not stable, since it tended to oscillate. As a consequence, penetration performance was reduced.
>
> We are certain that large numbers of this weapon will soon be encountered on the Eastern Front.

Apparently, the US-built weapon galvanized officials at *Waffenamt* into action and being lightweight, simple and inexpensive to manufacture it complied with most of their criteria. But they considered the anti-armour performance

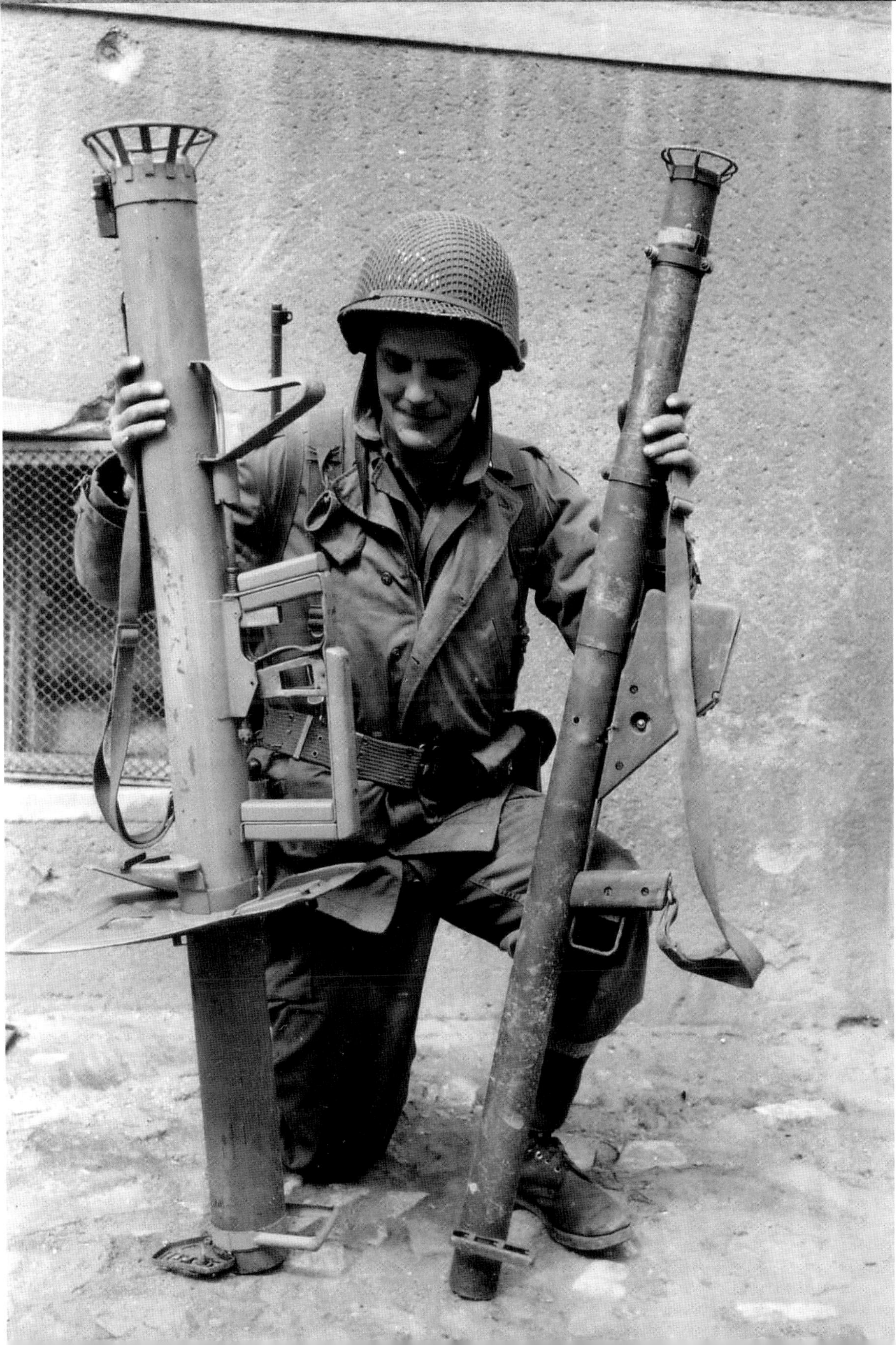

In September 1942, Benito Mussolini ordered the Italian army to send a complete Corps of three *Alpini* (mountain Infantry) divisions – *Tridentina*, *Julia* and *Cuneense* – to support German forces advancing on the Caucasus. Here two *Alpini* man a Swiss-built 4.7cm Böhler anti-tank gun.

to be inadequate, and subsequently ordered the size of the projectile to be increased to 8.8cm.

In April 1943, *Waffenamt* officials presented designs for three different types to *Reichsminister* Albert Speer, secretary for armament and ammunition:

Comment:

Two of the weapons presented were selected for production:

1). 7.5cm *Rückstossfreie Kanone* [RfK – recoilless gun] 43

2). 8.8cm *Raketenwerfer* [RW – rocket-powered weapon] 43

The 8.8cm *Raketenwerfer* (RakWrf – rocket launcher) 43 was developed in parallel to the RaKPzB 54 *Panzerschreck*, but although having a comparable performance the type was much heavier and more complex to produce.

A third weapon, the 8.8cm *RaketenPanzerbüchse* (RPzB) [based on the Bazooka] is not yet ready. The ammunition requires further development work.
7.5cm RfK 43
Recoilless gun with rifled barrel, cartridge ammunition, spin stabilized.
Advantages: Low weight of 40kg in two loads; low firing height.
Disadvantages: Insufficient penetration (100mm). Problems with ammunition production which will result in a reduction in the production of ammunition for

the infantry gun. A powerful and dangerous exhaust blast when fired, this could also reveal the position of the gun.

8.8cm RW 43

Rocket gun; smooth bore; fin-stabilized cartridge ammunition.

Advantages: Good penetration performance (130mm to 150mm). Allegedly there are no problems since there seems to be more than adequate production capacity. The cartridge requires only 60g of propellant against 240g for the RfK 43. The ammunition is similar to that of the RakPzB. The weapon is easy and efficient to operate.

Disadvantages: Weight with wheels 130kg, without 96kg and has to be transported in four loads. An attempt to reduce the weight to 60kg by using a split-trail carriage failed, which resulted in a lack of stability when during firing.

8.8cm RPzB

Recoilless rocket weapon (*Ofenrohr* – stove pipe); smooth bore; fin-stabilized cartridge ammunition.

Advantages: Low weight (9.5kg), one-man operation, very simple construction and can be positioned anywhere. Simple to mass produce.

Disadvantages: Development of the ammunition is yet to be completed, but should be available in two months.

Due to being fitted with an artillery-type breech block, the RakWrf 43 was easier to load and much safer to operate. The weapon was hand aimed and man-portable but, in reality, it was far less mobile than a *Panzerschreck*.

Conclusion:

After careful evaluation of the above, the 8.8cm RakPzB is considered to be the ideal close-range armour-piercing weapon for the infantry. All means must be employed to expedite the development of this weapon and begin production.

On examining the other weapons, the 8.8cm RakWrf 43 was chosen despite it being heavier which classes it as light anti-tank gun. The deciding factor was it having better penetration performance and the readily available production capacity for the ammunition. Finally, it could be put into production immediately and is a viable alternative until the RakPzB 54 is ready.

[Note. The term cartridge ammunition is misleading: the fins on the projectile were kept folded by a wrap-around cover which remained in the barrel after firing.]

The *Raketenwerfer* (RW) 43, called '*Puppchen*' (puppy) by troops, was to be the first of the types to be developed and delivered to front-line forces.

It is interesting to note that the RW 43 was regarded as a purely transitional weapon until the *Panzerschreck* became available.

8.8cm *Raketenwerfer* 43

In August 1943, production of the 8.8cm RW 43 began and two series, each of 3,000 weapons, were planned. In October 1943, the *Waffenamt* accepted the first batch and delivered the majority to the army, but also supplied 732 to a number of (unknown) units.

The script from a lecture by the *Organisationsabteilung*, dated September 1943, clearly states: 'Production of the second series is to be cancelled because

8.8cm RW 43

Calibre	8.8cm
Barrel length	1,600mm
Effective range (maximum)	700m
Muzzle velocity	110mps
Rate of fire	10rpm
Barrel's life span (est)	1,000 rounds
Weight with wheels	149kg
Weight without wheels	105kg
Armour penetration	160mm

the development of a new anti-tank weapon, with superior performance, has been initiated.

The *Waffenamt* lists the number of these weapons in service with frontline and replacement units, but the number remains unchanged for the first half of 1944. No losses have been noted, so it seems most unlikely that these weapons were ever used in combat. From June 1944, the number in service began to be gradually reduced.

The RW 43 was a simple assembly: a gun-type barrel, fitted with an armoured gun shield, mounted on a lower carriage fitted with two wheels. The rocket barrel was fitted with a simple breech block, but had no elevating or side traversing gear; the weapon was aimed manually. The breech block

The RaKWrf 43 was technically quite similar to the 2.8cm *schwere Panzerbüchse* (s PzB – heavy anti-tank rifle) 41. Here the loader places a round in the breech ready for the gunner to aim and fire.

A tank destroyer team from PzGrenDiv Grossdeutschland: the loader has inserted the rocket-powered projectile and is fitting the firing plug into the electrical socket. Note, the weapon is fitted with a gun shield to protect the gunner from the rocket blast. (Getty)

	8.8cm RPzB 54	8.8cm RPzB 54/1
Calibre	8.8cm	8.8cm
Barrel length	1,640mm	1,350mm
Effective range (maximum)	150m	180m
Muzzle velocity	110mps	110mps
Rate of fire	4–5rpm	5rpm
Barrel's life span (est)	1,000 rounds	1,000 rounds
Weight with shield	11kg	9.6kg
Armour penetration	160mm	160mm

had a considerable effect on the range, but the substantial single trail-type gun carriage only absorbed a minimal amount of the powerful recoil. A small drawbar could be attached to the carriage so that the gun could be moved by the crew or pulled by a horse, but it was too fragile to be towed by any type of motor vehicle. Lowering the firing height was simply achieved by removing the wheels. In winter conditions the gun could be mounted on snow skids.

The RW 43 was considered to be a stationary weapon, any change of position under fire was only possible if the battlefield was obscured by smoke or weather conditions; this considerably reduced combat effectiveness. It was ordered that the RW 43 was never to be deployed unless two or more guns were available to a combat unit.

Some 4,300 of the type were manufactured, but the 8.8cm RW 43 is never mentioned in documentation from December 1943 to the end of the war.

Despite the RW 43 being considered to be an interim weapon, until the RPzB was ready for production, the GenStbdH asked the *Waffenamt* to initiate the design of an advanced version in 1943:

Combat range (maximum):	800m
Armour penetration:	150mm
Weight:	less than 500kg

No further information has been found for this project.

Organization

The front-line deployment of the 8.8cm RW 43 cannot be confirmed, and the author can so far find no information as to whether this rocket launcher was issued to any combat units.

The obvious difference between the cost of manufacturing a *Puppchen* and a *Panzerschreck* made the cancellation of the RW 43 inevitable. Another factor was that the RPzB 54 and the *Faustpatrone*, which could be produced quickly and also in very large numbers, were beginning to enter service. Military planners did not lose any sleep after writing-off the *Puppchen*.

A *Panzerjäger* unit has built a dummy tank from logs and sheathed it with armour plates, of different thickness and quality, as target for anti-tank teams training to use man-portable weapons.

RPzB 54 and 54/1

The *Raketen-Panzerbüchse*, was designed as a man-portable recoilless anti-tank weapon and basically an enlarged copy of a US-built Bazooka. Like many weapons the RPzB was also given a 'pet' name by front-line troops: *Pusterohr* (peashooter), *Ofenrohr* (stove pipe) or *Panzerschreck* (tank shock),

The weapon was almost identical to a Bazooka but fired an 8.8cm projectile which required a more powerful propellant. The exhaust flame from the rear of the barrel threatened not only the loader but also the gunner. The operating manual for the RPzB 54, instructs the gunner to wear a gas mask (without filter), the issued protective hood, a steel helmet and also a pair of thick gloves. The loader was instructed to keep his head out of the way as the weapon fired.

Capable of firing high-explosive or armour-piercing ammunition, the 2cm FlaK was a much-feared weapon. In 1943, a wooden *Behelfslafette* was designed to allow the gun to be deployed as a ground weapon.

The 8.8cm *Raketen-Panzerbüchse-Granat* (RPzBGr) 4322 projectile was very similar to the rocket used for the *Puppchen*, but it was ignited electrically, whereas the RW 43 used a conventional firing pin.

In October 1943, the RPzB was put into production with numbers increasing to achieve a target of 50,000 a month by December.

When the RPzB entered service, it was given the suffix 54 as an identifier. Like many previous new weapons, it was plagued with a number of problems which would have to be solved by front-line units. One simple solution made by many units was to fabricate a basic blast shield to avoid burn injuries.

In January 1944, a purpose-designed blast shield became a standard fitting on all production RPzB 54. But the shield, along with the long barrel, made the weapon extremely cumbersome to handle. A plan to shorten the length of the barrel was realized when a new projectile, powered by a propellant with a shorter burn time and no loss in ballistic performance, became available. The short-barrel version was designated RaKPzB 54/1 and deliveries began in March 1944.

In December 1944, a series of trials began in the search for a more powerful propellant to increase ballistic performance velocity from 110mps to 160mps to improve the effective range. No information has been found to confirm whether this work was completed.

Organization

As soon as the new anti-tank weapons left the factory they were delivered, by all means available, and with some urgency, to front-line units.

All of the new *Panzerzerstör-Bataillone* (PzZerstBtl – tank destroyer battalions) were to be established in the same way as those PzJgAbt and s PzJgAbt on army level. The PzZerstBtl were to be deployed as a dedicated defensive force to protect front-line positions from attack by enemy armour.

In September 1943, the GenStbdH decided on the allocation of the new anti-tank weapons:

I request the following to be issued:

I. *Ofenrohr* (with six projectiles each)

a.) For PzZerstBtl (150 per battalion)
HGr *Süd*	450
HGr *Mitte*	450
HGr *Nord*	450
HGr 'A'	150

	Panzerschreck	Panzerfaust
InfDiv, VGrDiv, Lw FeldDiv	300	2,700
SS KavDiv	130	2,700
JägDiv, GebJägDiv	200	2,700
FallschJägDiv ground service	200	2,700
FallschJägDiv airborne service	300	2,700
PzDiv	130	1,400
PzGrenDiv	120	1,600

b.) For *Armee-Waffenschulen* (Armee WaffSch – army weaponry school)

HGr *Süd*   400
HGr *Mitte*   400
HGr *Nord*   200
HGr 'A'   100

c.) For *Grenadier-Kompanien (30 per division)*

HGr *Süd*   1,750
HGr *Mitte*   1,500
HGr *Nord*   1,250
HGr 'A'   250

The army groups are responsible for the distribution.

II. *Puppchen* (projectors only)

a.) For *Armee-Waffenschulen*

HGr *Süd*   120
HGr *Mitte*   120
HGr *Nord*   60
HGr 'A'   30

b.) For InfPzJgKp (15 approx.)

HGr *Süd*   1,000
HGr *Mitte*   850
HGr *Nord*   700
HGr 'A'   120

The army groups are responsible for the distribution.

An NCO instructs men from an infantry unit on how to operate a *kleine Faustpatrone* (small fist charge) the smallest type of *Panzerfaust* (tank fist). To operate, the weapon was first unlocked and cocked, the gun sight raised and the right-hand thumb placed on the trigger.

III. *Faustpatronen*

a.) For each PzZerstBtl   150 pcs
b.) For each WaffSch   100 pcs

In a document dated December 1943, the OKH noted that the PzZerstBtl were to receive 216 *Ofenrohr* supplied with 2,160 projectiles. Most infantry divisions were not even considered at that time, only those being in combat in focal flash points were to receive 200 *Ofenrohr* and a supply of 2,000 projectiles.

But this would only happen after production of the weapon had reached a sufficient level that would allow all divisions to be issued with a similar number.

The *Ofenrohre* (and *Faustpatronen*) were to be issued to those units as an additional weapon, and subsequently were not covered in any KStN structures.

In January 1945, the following targets were adopted:

	Panzerschreck	Panzerfaust
InfDiv, VGrDiv, Lw FeldDiv	300	2,700
SS-KavDiv	130	2,700
JägDiv, GebJägDiv	200	2,700
FallschJägDiv (land)	200	2,700
FallschJägDiv (airborne)	300	2,700
PzDiv	130	1,400
PzGrenDiv	120	1,600

Faustpatrone

Sometime before the development of the *Panzerschreck* was started, work on a much simpler hand-held weapon had been initiated.

After preliminary trials in December 1942, the first pre-production version of this revolutionary weapon had been completed. At first it was known as

A *Panzerfaust* 60 rocket-powered projectile: The fins would be folded as the projectile was loaded and since it was delivered in ready-to-use condition it did not require a fuse. (Getty)

	Panzerfaust 30 (klein)	Panzerfaust 30 (groß)	Panzerfaust 60	Panzerfaust 100	Panzerfaust 150
Diameter of projectile	10.5cm	15cm	15cm	15cm	?
Effective Range (maximum)	30m	30m	60m	100m	150m
Muzzle velocity	30mps	30mps	45mps	62mps	82mps
Weight	11kg	9.6kg			
Armour penetration	140mm	200mm	200mm	200mm	200mm

the *Faustpatrone klein* (fist charge small) 30, but it was renamed *Panzerfaust* (armoured fist) a short time later.

This weapon consisted of a short firing tube with a 10cm shaped-charge projectile which was propelled by a charge fixed in the tube. The weapon was fitted with a rudimentary gunsight and a simple trigger mechanism. After firing the weapon was simply discarded. Data states that it could penetrate 140mm of steel at a range of 30m.

At the same time the *Faustpatrone* entered production, the more powerful *Panzerfaust* 30 (*groß* – large), fitted with a 14.9cm warhead, was under development.

In March 1943, both types were successfully demonstrated to the *Heereswaffenamt* at Kummersdorf and subsequently ordered into production. As a comparison, a captured Bazooka was fired and showed that it had much better accuracy and range than the *Panzerfaust*. German military planners initiated the development of the *Panzerschreck*.

In July 1943, a total of 3,000 *Panzerfaust klein* and 3,000 *Panzerfaust* 30 were sent to the Eastern Front for troop trials. In October 1943, both were ordered into mass production at an expected rate of 100,000 *Panzerfaust klein* and 200,000 *Panzerfaust* 30 each month. But due to a lack of manpower and ever-present shortage of raw materials this ambitious rate was not attained until mid-1944.

While the production of the two types was being ramped up, an even more powerful version was under development. The *Panzerfaust* 60 was fitted with a 14.9cm warhead and had improved propellant charge, which allowed the effective range to increase from 30m to 60m.

In November 1944, the *Panzerfaust* 100 was ready for production. The weapon was fitted with a 14.9cm warhead and had an even more powerful propellant, which improved the range from 60m to 100m.

In April 1944, in response to an earlier request from the army for an anti-infantry projectile, the German munitions industry developed the *Splitterfaust*

(fragmentation fist) warhead; but this was rejected by the army in favour of a fragmentation ring which was simply slipped over a hollow-charge projectile when needed.

Some two months later, the even more improved *Panzerfaust* 150 had completed development trials. It fired a 10.6cm projectile which, although lighter, had much better aerodynamics and range was increased to 150m. Operating the type was much improved; the simple trigger was replaced by a pistol-type grip and the weapon, in order to save steel, was reloadable.

Although some 100,000 had been produced by April 1945, none were delivered to those defending the Fatherland. Surprisingly, the development of the more advanced *Panzerfaust* 250 had been initiated with production planned for August 1945.

Interestingly, the *Heereswaffenamt* carried out a series of firing trials with captured British and US Army shaped-charge anti-tank weapons. A report was issued that showed 90mm of armour was penetrated by a Bazooka, whereas the British PIAT penetrated 120mm.

At the beginning of 1944, *General der Infanterie* was requested, by the department of the secretary for ammunitions, to decide whether the *Faustpatrone* or the *Panzerschreck* should continue in production. The general

Spring 1945 in Hungary: A German anti-tank team armed with *Panzerfaust* prepare to establish a defensive position to halt, or at least delay, rapidly advancing Russian forces.

A *Fallschirmjäger* (paratroop) unit takes cover
in the shadow of an abandoned M4A3 Sherman.
One carries a RakPzB 54, another a *Panzerfaust* 60
and two are armed with a *Maschinenpistole* (MP40
– machine pistol) with the shoulder butt extended.

declined, since he did not have sufficient information from units using the weapons on the frontline. However, documents show that the production of *Panzerschreck* was halted at some time between August and September 1944. But other records show that production recommenced in October 1944; possibly due to the dire situation faced by German defenders on all fronts. It is thought that production of both weapons continued until end of the war.

In 1944, a further establishment post was created and introduced on army level. The *Stabsoffizier für die Panzerbekämpfung* (staff officer for anti-tank defence) was to oversee all anti-tank units, the weapons, and their training and reconnaissance within each respective army. The GenInspdPzTrp as the officer responsible for anti-tank weapons published a pamphlet:

Mission
Anti-tank defence has become the number one deciding issue in this war. All weapons must be deployed effectively.

The leaflet went on to demand a commitment for all available anti-tank weapons to be centralized. He made a demand for all personnel to be trained in every detail of anti-tank defence.

The introduction of RakPzB 54 and *Faustpatrone* into service was not a straightforward process as noted in this report submitted by the *Waffenschule* (weapon training school) of PzAOK 1:

On 3 November 1943, a test firing using RakPzB 54 (*Ofenrohr* and *Faustpatrone*) at a captured Russian T-34 was performed.
Result:
Oberleutnant von Majewski (OKH/*Waffenamt*) using an *Ofenrohr*, fired 12 rounds at a range of 100m. He scored three hits: the first one penetrated the 4cm armour adjacent to the front running wheel; this would have been fatal for the entire crew. The second hit penetrated the 6cm thick turret side and the 1cm thick armour of the gun sleeve. Again, the complete crew would have been killed. His third round penetrated the open turret hatch and detonated in a field near the tank.
Seven projectiles missed the target, either to the left or right, and the remaining two were duds.
To summarize, the trajectory of the projectiles was very erratic, but there is a rumour that the latest ammunition will have better accuracy.
We achieved very good results when firing the *Faustpatrone*. All three hit the target at 30m range, and effectively penetrated the armour. Just the detonation of the weapon would have neutralized the tank crew.
Another *Faustpatrone* penetrated the 15cm amour of the turret cupola.

Almost simultaneously, a *Sturm-Battailon* in PzAOK 1 submitted an after-action report:

On 3 November 1943, the *Ofenrohr* and *Faustpatrone* were used against enemy tanks for the first time.

During a night intrusion by enemy forces, we fired 20 projectiles from four *Ofenrohr* at three T-34 tanks that were entering a village behind our front-line positions. We are sufficiently satisfied that each tank was hit several times, but surprisingly all tanks remained mobile and continued to fight.

On another occasion, we opened fire on several T-34 tanks at 60m to 150m range, and scored several hits. But once again none were immobilized. On both occasions the *Ofenrohr* were operated by well-trained and experienced gunners.

Firing at night is most difficult for the gunner since wearing a gas mask impedes his ability to aim the weapon.

Many gunners have suffered burns to the face and hands from exhaust blast, this is despite wearing a protective hood, heavy gloves and gas mask as ordered. The design of the aiming device is too simple and is very is easily damaged; this must be improved.

During an assault by the battalion over open terrain on 31 October, it was found that the *Ofenrohr* is not an attack weapon. The gunners are hampered by the weight of the ammunition and cannot keep pace: also the brightly-coloured ammunition crates are highly visible.

Test firing an *Ofenrohr* at a destroyed T-34, showed that the gunner was unable to hit the target with any reliability at range of 50m. When a projectile did hit the target, it created a hole 1cm in diameter.

It also proved to be very difficult to achieve hits with the *Faustpatrone*. Two clear hits were achieved on the T-34, but neither penetrated the armour.

These reports indicate that both the *Panzerfaust* and *Panzerschreck* had not been sufficiently developed for use as a front-line anti-tank weapon.

But work was continuing apace to produce more effective ammunition with improved accuracy and explosive impact. Military officials even addressed the question of operating safety.

The *Faustpatrone* would soon become a most popular weapon with anti-tank combat teams; it was easy to operate and had a good accuracy, even at maximum range. The armour penetration performance of the warhead was comparable to the HaftHl 3kg. There had been problems with the impact fuse, but these were quickly rectified.

The following combat report was submitted by GrenRgt 260 and illustrates the dangers faced by German troops when confronted by a massed attack by the Red Army:

A German infantryman armed with a *Panzerfaust* 60 bravely waits in his foxhole for an enemy tank to come within range.

Report on the probation of *große Faustpatrone 2*

At 10:00hrs on 14 November 1943, the Russian launched his third attack of the day. A large number of their infantry was being carried on tanks. When these came within 300m to 400m of our lines, we opened fire and successfully eliminated one densely packed group; the rest jumped down from the tanks and continued to advance. After breaking through the barbed wire, one of the leading T-34s passed alongside trench No.1, and *Oberfeldwebel* Schweikert (11./GrenRgt 260) fired his *Faustpatrone* and scored a hit on the side of the turret leaving a 4cm to 5cm diameter hole. The tank halted, but then began to move off; but did not fire its main gun or machine gun. *Gefreiter* Gruner jumped up and threw an incendiary bottle [Molotov cocktail]. The crew then began to escape in panic and were shot.

The next day another T-34 passed close to trench No.1 and Schweikert tried to fire a *Faustpatrone* at the hull, but the weapon failed. We fired a total of 11 projectiles, but only one reached its target. After the battle was over we initiated an investigation. Apparently, the reported failures of the *Faustpatronen* were due to errors made by the operator.

Front-line troops soon learned how to use their new anti-tank weapon and this was reflected in subsequent experience reports. became better.

On 18 November 1943, an after-action report was submitted by 6.*Armee*:

To *Heeresgruppe* 'A'
Faustpatrone
Because of it being easy to handle and its powerful explosive impact on the target, the *Faustpatrone* (*groß*) has become very popular with our combat teams. Only a short period of practice is necessary to achieve high accuracy; even a soldier firing the weapon for the first time had only a few misses. Firing trials at a captured T-34 resulted in the 15cm armour being penetrated even at an unfavourable angle of impact.

The preferred deployment of the new anti-tank weapon *Panzer-Zerstör-Bataillone* (PzZerstBtl – tank destroyer battalions) was soon deemed to be disadvantageous.

In April 1944, a report was received from AOK 18:

1) One should be clear that the quality of our infantry will not be the same as it was in 1941/42. The standard of training has significantly decreased.

2) During recent defensive battles, the 2cm FlaK has proven to be a very effective weapon. The guns were positioned some 200m to the rear of our battle lines for safety. Russian infantry is extremely vulnerable to high-explosive fire and as a result even a massed assault could be easily defeated. For this reason, we demand the establishment of 2cm FlaK battalions at army troop level.

3) The PzerZerstBtl did not prove effective. In combat, on many occasions the situation required deployment of a single section to assist an infantry unit. A commitment in battalion strength was impossible, since it could not be resupplied in combat. A number of the weapons were lost and the gunners were absorbed into infantry units. Our losses mounted until both battalions were annihilated.

4) The *Ofenrohr* continues to cause many injuries. The *Faustpatrone* has proven to be effective, but it we must be aware that many weapons will get lost during any retreat. Our infantry continues to demand the deployment of a mobile PaK [*Sturmgeschütz*].

As the war entered its final phases the German military was forced to conscript younger men, many having recently completed their education. Here are two young-looking soldiers, one armed with a *Panzerfaust* 60, the other carrying a standard issue *Karabiner* (K – carbine) 98. Although designed as an anti-tank weapon, the *Panzerfaust* was also highly effective against buildings. (Getty)

On 17 June 1944, the high command of *Heeresgruppe Südukraine* (army group south Ukraine) also reported on the commitment of PzZerstBtl, but with some reservations:

1) The PzZerstBtl is a valuable anti-tank reserve at army level due to it being highly mobile. For this reason, they can be deployed quickly to establish an anti-tank defence at a focal point on the battlefront.
2) The PzZerstBtl have proven to be especially effective in difficult and obscured terrain, in areas where no or only a few anti-tank guns are deployed and also during the hours of darkness. They are considered to be a vital element in the divisional anti-tank defence.
3) During longer breaks in the fighting, men of the PzZerstBtl trained a number of troops in the grenadier regiment to operate the *Ofenrohr* and *Faustpatrone*.

It is difficult to determine which point of view was correct for meeting the demands of the struggling infantry on the Eastern and all other fronts.

However, the availability of potent anti-tank weapons at the lowest level – the grenadier in his trench – seems to be essential. This point of view is supported by the new organizational structures.

The '1944'-type Divisions

In 1944, a number of completely revised organizational structures were introduced. These show that the basic organization of tank destroyer units were to be standardized as *Infanteriedivision* (infantry division) 44, the *Gebirgsdivision* (mountain division) 44 and the *Jägerdivision* (anti-tank division) 44.

At regimental level, 36 *Ofenrohr* (RakPzB 54/1) and three s PaK (towed) were to be supplied. The divisional PzJgAbt was issued with ten *Sturmgeschütz*, (alternatively *leichte Panzerjäger* [le PzJg – light tank hunter] IV or le PzJg 38) and/or 14 s PaK (self-propelled or towed) and/or 12 FlaK guns (self-propelled or towed).

As in the past, the lack of new and replacement equipment meant that there could be a significant variation in the numbers (and types) indicated.

Panzer division 44 had two companies, each supplied with ten or 14 le PzJg IV in the PzJgAbt and also six s PaK (Sfl) in the PzGrenRegt.

The PzGrenDiv 44 was issued with two companies each equipped with ten or 14 le PzJg IV in the PzJgAbt and four s PaK at the regimental level.

	8.8cm RakPzB 54			8.8cm RakWrf 43			Faustpatrone (all versions)		
				Numbers given according *Rüststand* statistics					
	Built	Available	Front losses	Built	Available	Front losses	Built	Available	Consumption
October 1943	2,340	0	0	732	0	0	50,000	6,000	500
November 1943	14,050	2,340	3	990	732	?	60,000	34,000	3,800
December 1943	16,265	16,387	35	1,531	1,722	?	96,000	82,500	20,600
January 1944	32,740	32,617	8	1,050	3,252	1	84,000	148,600	8,500
February 1944	35,075	65,349	25	0	4,302	?	124,400	220,600	33,200
March 1944	73,851	100,399	172	0	4,302	?	119,000	255,000	109,000
April 1944	27,580	174,131	97	0	4,302	?	196,000	250,700	32,300
May 1944	32,860	201,561	196	0	4,302	?	164,000	368,500	50,000
June 1944	24,820	233,814	106	0	4,295	7	166,000	471,700	50,000
July 1944	27,970	258,528	701	0	4,295	0	120,000	545,900	200,000
August 1944	0	185,797	814	0	3,009	16	263,000	539,000	318,000
September 1944	0	284,983	2,786	0	2,990	19	294,000	876,700	220,000
October 1944	785	194,854	2,250	0	1,966	130	425,000	1,019,000	260,000
November 1944	1,289	193,763	2,876	0	1,836	62	280,000	998,000	250,000
December 1944	1,015	193,219	1,833	0	1,764	103	854,000	1,717,000	89,000
January 1945	12,520	150,977	2,117	0	1,661	10	981,000	2,054,000	507,000
February 1945	13,224	130,149	1,838	0	1,651	2	732,000	2,508,000	100,000
March 1945	?	139,730	?	0	1,649	?	776,000	3,018,000	150,000
April 1945	?	?	?	0	?	?	?	?	?
May 1945	?	?	?	0	?	?	?	?	?
Totals:		316,384			4,303			5,784,400	

Volksgrenadier-Divisions

In the summer of 1944, the collapse of *Heeresgruppe Mitte* and the D-Day landings invasion in Normandy would lead to the establishment of *Volks-Grenadier-Divisionen*. Although formed as standard infantry divisions, they had six instead of the usual nine battalions.

Each *Grenadier-Kompanie* (GrenKp – grenadier company) was issued with two *Zug* (platoons) armed with the *Sturmgewehr* (assault rifle) 44. The heavy company in a grenadier battalion had two heavy *Maschinengewehr* (MG – machine gun) platoons, an infantry gun platoon, equipped with four 7.5cm *leichte Infanterie Geschütze* (le IG – light infantry gun), and a mortar platoon equipped with six 8cm *Granate-Werfer* (GrWrf – grenade launcher) 34. At regimental level, the 13.Kp had two platoons each equipped with four 12cm GrWrf 42 each and an artillery platoon with four 7.5cm le IG.

Old and disabled men were recruited as 'soldiers' for the *Volkssturm* (people's militia), formed as the last line of defence in the German Reich. Here a member of the SS, wearing a *Eisernes Kreuz* (EK – iron cross) 1st class, trains his men in the use of the *Panzerfaust* 60 as they prepare to defend Berlin. (Getty)

The (14.) InfPzJgKp was dropped and replaced by a *Panzer-Zerstörer-Kompanie* (PzZerstKp – tank destroyer company) equipped with 36 RakPz 54/1.

All GrenKp were supplied with unknown numbers of *Faustpatronen/Panzerfaust*.

When enemy tanks launched an attack, the first weapons to open fire were the light infantry guns, but since they lacked armour penetration they were aimed at the side of the hull or the running gear. As the assault developed, they would be attacked by *Ofenrohr* in positions staggered along the length of the frontline. *Panzerfaust* were used in any emergency situation.

The level of mobility was very low, especially when compared to that for British or US forces. Where they were well supplied with motor transport, many German units were issued with bicycles and a number relied on horses.

The situation on the southern front in Italy was much different from that in Soviet Union. The wide-open terrain of the far east of Europe was the ideal battleground for highly-mobile armoured warfare. The *Wehrmacht* had perfected this type of action and remained dominant until end of 1942, when the Red Army, having learned to adopt less expansive tactics, began to counterattack in force despite previous horrendous losses. But the Red Army seemed to have an endless supply of equipment and manpower, which allowed them to establish formidably effective defensive lines.

In Italy, the rugged terrain in and around mountain areas caused many problems for German armoured units; the tanks could not be deployed using proven tactics and many suffered mechanical breakdowns, as did all motorized units. Brake and final drive units on tanks and assault guns items tended to fail. Subsequently, recovery teams were in constant demand and field workshop were hopelessly overburdened. The *Panzerjäger* were faced with the same problem, particularly with their heavy self-propelled guns. The troop avoided using the half-tracked tractor and, whenever possible, opted for a standard cargo truck. The self-propelled artillery, although their vehicles were much lighter than a tank, suffered similar breakdowns.

Constantly threatened by Allied artillery and ever-present Allied aircraft, *Heeresgruppe* 'C' was forced to react rather than act.

A short report submitted by 29.PzGrenDiv, describes their combat, from 16 to 20 December 1944, against British Commonwealth troops:

> 3. The New Zealander defends mainly from positions inside buildings. Snipers firing from the upper floors were extremely dangerous to our unexpectant infantry.
>
> 7. Like the MP 44, the *Faustpatrone* has proven to be a most important close-combat weapon against an enemy positioned in a building. Every grenadier must be thoroughly trained in the use of these weapons.

A *Volkssturm* anti-tank team, armed with a *Panzerfaust* 60, has constructed a bunker from the debris of surrounding buildings. Many of this aged force perished in their attempts to defend Berlin against the Red Army. (Getty)

After Kursk – on the Defensive 6

After the Allied invasion of Sicily (10 July 1943), German military officials were forced to cancel the planned offensive to take the Kursk salient. Consequently, the Red Army was now able to draw on what appeared to be an endless supply of reserves, forcing both *Heeresgruppe Mitte* and *Heeresgruppe Süd* to begin a long withdrawal. The German army had lost the initiative almost instantly, and had no reserves to launch a counterattack; all future battles would be fought to defend a 'controlled' retreat.

In 1943, although effective weapons were available to the *Panzerjäger*, they still faced a number of difficulties. Weighing more than 4,500kg, the newly introduced 8.8cm PaK had reached all limitations. The crews complained that the guns were far too heavy to move, and had to hope that a sufficient number of prime movers were available or even mobile. Guns were easily moved when the ground was firm, but mud or snow caused much difficulty. The constant shortage of prime movers frequently led to, occasionally, extremely high losses which were considered to be avoidable. This fact was confirmed by *Oberst* Klar of 18.*Armee* in January 1944:

> In the area controlled by 18.*Armee*, a total of 130 s PaK were lost. Main reason: a serious lack of suitable tractors

On a separate occasion, 70 newly-delivered 8.8cm PaK 43/41 had to destroyed with explosives because no prime movers were available.

Due to the size and excessive weight of the weapon, *Panzerjäger* units equipped with the 8.8cm PaK had to rely on its impressive long-range performance. If a crew positioned their gun in accordance with

The Ardelt-Rheinmetall *Waffenträger* (weapon carrier) was purpose-designed and cost-effective to manufacture. The 8.8cm PaK 43 was mounted on a flat-top chassis built using PzKpfw 38(t) parts and protected by an all-around gun shield. The vehicle did not enter production.

instructions, then should be possible to change position. Wherever the gun was positioned it would always be vulnerable to enemy artillery or a ground-attack aircraft.

Especially for the s PaK with its considerable shorter ranges new solutions were demanded.

PaK on '*Pilz*'

The general retreat on the Eastern Front forced German military officials to adapt their battle strategy and subsequently order field commanders to establish and hold defensive positions.

Although lacking sufficient armour protection, the first self-propelled anti-tank gun gave the *Panzerjager* units sufficient mobility to fight in virtually all battlefield conditions. But what they really required was a heavily armoured type such as a *Sturmgeschütz* (later *Jagdpanzer*), but this would take some time. The first infantry units were issued with *Sturmgeschütz* in 1943, as an integral part of their *Panzerjäger-Abteilung*.

The situation called for simple solutions to the problems facing the *Panzerjäger* to be found as a matter of some urgency. As a result, the *Waffenamt* accelerated the design and development of a number of new projects.

Aware of the ever-present shortage of tractors, they ordered the design of a dismountable gun which could be carried on a vehicle. All available types of vehicle were to be examined to see if they could be cost effectively modified. All would be fitted with a simple manually operated gantry-type crane to dismount the gun.

A simple *Sockel* (pedestal-type mounting – for some reason it was also referred to as '*Pilz*' [mushroom]) – was designed and bolted to the carrier vehicle. This pedestal mount carried the weapon, which could be fired from the carrier. All around traverse was obligatory. This combination could be dug in a temporary gun position resulting in a low fire height. A change of gun position was less problematic, since no tractor had to be fetched from behind. The half or fully-tracked carriers had a superior mobility in rough terrain anyway.

When firm fronts had to be established, the gun including its *Sockel* could be dismounted. Simple trails were fixed to the pedestal mount resulting in a very low profile. The gun could be easily dug in, maintaining its all-around traverse. The carrier vehicle could be withdrawn for other applications; it was then used for moving or towing other weapons or for transporting ammunition to the position. Having in mind the tense German production

reality, this approach seems to be understandable. When the situation so required, the gun could be picked up again.

However, facing determined enemy attacks precious material could not be recovered leading to total loss.

Although attempts were undertaken to generalize the ground mounts for different guns, the few realized solutions were not identical.

During a presentation to the Führer on 14 September 1943 the following ideas were suggested:

a) Development of an le FH 18/40 with 360-degrees traverse on an SdKfz 11, dismountable with a cruciform-type carriage.

b) Development using a 7.5cm PaK 44 (L/70) with 360-degrees traverse on an SdKfz 11 dismountable with a cruciform-type carriage.

c) Development of a le PaK 40 with 360-degrees traverse on an RSO, dismountable with cruciform-type carriage.

This trial vehicle of the 7.5cm PaK 40/4 auf RSO is tested in a simulated inclined position. The gun could be fired from the vehicle with a traverse of 360 degrees or dismounted by using a small crane fitted on the vehicle. The gun would then be placed on a flat cruciform-type carriage and used as a static anti-tank weapon. The tractor element could be used for other purposes.

Some 80 of the light self-propelled anti-tank guns were built using the RSO chassis and mounting a 7.5cm PaK 41/4. A total of 42 cartridge-type shells could be carried in a bay under the cargo bed. The Sfl was too slow and far too loud and did not prove effective.

d) Development of an le FHG 18/40 with 360-degrees traverse on PzKpfw III/IV chassis, dismountable with cruciform-type carriage.

All developments 'a' to 'd' shall be designed in such a way that all parts are interchangeable. This will ease manufacture, maintenance and also the supply of spare parts.

Two weeks later, a meeting was held in the presence of Hitler and Speer to discuss armaments, in particular the two projects for the *Panzerjäger*:

7.5cm PaK 44 on SdKfz 11

In 1943, it was decided to mount a 7.5cm PaK 44 L/70 on a modified SdKfz 11 half-track vehicle; a simple and very straightforward process. A PaK 44 (later re-designated PaK 42) similar to the 7.5cm KwK 42 L/70 mounted in a PzKpfw V Panther medium tank was to be fitted on the pedestal-type gun mount. The method for dismounting the gun would be decided after troop and field trials. The vehicle did not have any armour protection for the driver, but the engine compartment was fitted with an armoured cover. The PaK 44 was fitted with an armoured gun shield.

A prototype was built, but the project was cancelled in early 1944. A small number (six) of an advanced version mounting a 10.5cm le FH 18/40 were produced and were used against Canadian troops in 1945. A small crane was fitted on the side of the vehicle to dismount the weapon.

7.5cm PaK 40/4 on RSO

The *Raupenschlepper Ost* (RSO – fully-tracked tractor East) was developed as a supply vehicle especially for deployment on the Eastern Front. Due to its undoubted mobility in deep mud or snow, the RSO was selected to mount a 7.5cm PaK 40.

The standard driver's cab was removed, and replaced with a simple steel assembly to protect the driver and co-driver; for combat the 'cab' was folded down over the seats.

The vehicle was demonstrated to Hitler during an armaments meeting, who said in a later speech that he was delighted and went on to emphasize its excellent mobility over all terrain and particularly in winter conditions.

He also viewed the '*Pilz*'-type gun mounting which he found 'a most promising design' and demanded development to be accelerated,

In January 1944, a 7.5cm PaK 40 auf RSO was demonstrated to Adolf Hitler at a gathering of the latest and proposed anti-tank weapons. The erratic steering on the RSO made it necessary to securely lash the gun down on two cradles.

as he wanted the device to be produced for the 7.5cm le FH, the 7.5cm PaK 42 and the 8.8cm PaK 43.

A pre-production batch of 60 (7.5cm PaK 40/4 auf RSO) had been completed by the end of 1943 and all were issued to units in *Heeresgruppe Mitte*.

While the mobility in rough terrain was in general acceptable, troops considered the vehicle to be far too slow and were unhappy at the lack of armour protection and interior space. When operating, engine revolutions (rpm) had to be kept high, which created a tremendous noise and made any movement near the frontline very dangerous; occasionally impossible. Troops had to be careful not to overloaded an RSO, past experiences had shown that this could cause the chassis to break.

A supply of ammunition (42 rounds) was carried under the cargo bed with more carried in a second RSO which also transported the crane and cruciform-type carriage.

Waffenträger

Hitler, who was completely aware of the overall situation on the Eastern Front, became obsessed by the idea of mounting all 7.5cm PaK 40 and 8.8cm PaK 43 being produced on self-propelled carriers. He had repeatedly demanded that all production of the respective towed versions must be cancelled.

So far only hulls of outdated tanks (PzKpfw II, PzKpfw III/IV, PzKpfw 38[t] and various captured types) had been modified, but many of the older types were mechanically unreliable. Hitler became more vitriolic in his communications to military planners when demanding the development of an improved self-propelled carriage.

Eventually, the design of a carrier chassis had been completed and work on producing a prototype commenced with much urgency. The type became known as the *Waffenträger* (weapon carrier) when field trials began. From the very beginning it had been planned to mount both anti-tank and artillery guns on the vehicle and for the running gear to be assembled from components being currently produced to simplify repair in the field and the supply of spare parts. The vehicle was designed to have a minimum ground clearance of 45cm and a maximum speed of 35kph on a hard-packed surface.

It was logical to mount the 8.8cm PaK 43 – as well as the 10.5cm le FH 18 – since the gun could also be successfully deployed as an artillery piece,

but the standard artillery-type sighting telescope must be supplemented with a panoramic gun sight.

Ardelt-Rheinmetall *Waffenträger*

To relieve the difficult circumstances surrounding the development of any new types, an ambitious engineer, *Oberst* Gunter Ardelt, proposed to manufacture a mechanically simple weapon carrier at the factory he owned in Eberswalde.

Ardelt had decided to use components from the proven PzKpfw 38(t), light tank. His design involved moving the engine to the front of the hull, releasing precious space in which to mount the gun. Rheinmetall modified the gun and fabricated a purpose-built shallow fully traversable turret (virtually an enclosed armour shield). When used as a field artillery, the gun could be elevated to a maximum of 45 degrees.

A sole *Versuchsfahrzeug* (trial vehicle) was completed by Ardelt.

Steyr *Waffenträger*

The situation was so desperate that another company, Steyr of Austria, was contracted to design and deliver their version. As the manufacturer of the

When the Ardelt-Rheinmetall *Waffenträger* (weapon carrier) project was cancelled, *Oberst* Ardelt began working on a simplified design. A trial run of 100 was authorized, but only seven had been delivered by February 1945.

Steyr of Austria was contracted to design a *Waffenträger* in cooperation with Krupp. It was to be built using RSO tractor components and armed with an 8.8cm PaK 43 L/71 anti-tank gun. The vehicle did not progress beyond the prototype stage.

RSO tractor they decided to utilize readily available components. The overall construction of their *Waffenträger* was almost identical to the Ardelt vehicle, but the gun and turret were developed by Krupp.

Again, only a trial vehicle was built.

Ardelt-Krupp *Waffenträger*

Both the Ardelt-Rheinmetall and Steyr types showed great promise and trials of their respective vehicles commenced in mid-1944. But, once again the constant shortage of materials, manufacturing capacity and also the dire economic situation in the Reich, caused the *Waffenamt* to issue a contract to Ardelt requesting them to produce another, but much simpler type of *Waffenträger*.

Although the specification was somewhat vague, Ardelt decided to design a smaller vehicle, again primarily utilizing components from a PzKpfw 38(t). Again, he decided to position the engine and transmission at the front of the chassis.

The result was a relatively small tracked vehicle which appeared to be nothing more than a flat-bed cargo carrier.

However, the earlier and more sophisticated *Waffenträger* had been fitted with a rotatable turret, but this latest version mounted a complete 8.8cm PaK 43 protected by a slightly enlarged gun shield.

The driver had only rudimentary armour protection to his front and sides, and the crew sat at the rear on foldable seats.

Although 100 of the '0'-series of *Waffenträger* Ardelt were ordered to be built, only seven had been completed by February 1945.

On 26 February 1945, the commander of *Heeresgruppe Weichsel* ordered that the surviving vehicles should be used to establish *Panzerjäger-Alarmkompanie* Eberswalde which was to be commanded by the now *Oberstleutnant* Ardelt. Many of his creations were used in the defence of his home town against the advancing Red Army.

Further *Waffenträger* concepts never progressed beyond the drawing board.

Festungs-PaK 7

Hitler, completely ignoring the conditions laid out in the Treaty of Versailles, decided to establish a system of fortifications to defend the western borders of the Reich. This line, which Hitler saw as being of both military and propaganda value, was called *Westwall* – Siegfried Line to the British.

The situation in the east was completely different. In 1934 the Nazi regime, not restricted by any treaties, ordered the construction of a system of fortifications – known as the *Ostwall* – stretching from the river Warta to the Oder as protection from Polish forces in the garrison city of Posen. But these had not been completed when German forces invaded and occupied the country in 1939. Consequently, all further construction work was cancelled.

After the invasion of The Low Countries and France, the defence of 'Fortress Europe' would become an important part of German strategic planning. In December 1941, Hitler boasted that he would build fortifications along more than 5,000km of coastline occupied by German forces. On 19 August 1942, British and Canadian forces launched Operation *Jubilee*, an amphibious assault landing at Dieppe,. The raid was a failure, but it spurred Hitler to order the construction of the *Atlantikwall* to begin immediately. During the following two years, a growing system of strongpoints and bunkers and were constructed to house all types of artillery, including naval and anti-tank weapons and FlaK guns. A number of bunkers would be fitted with a tank turret.

After the successful D-Day landings on 6 June 1944, the situation had totally changed. As German forces began their retreat, a decision was made

Many of the bunkers that formed the Atlantic Wall were equipped with obsolete weapons including the 5cm KwK L/42. Large numbers (some 1,800 were documented) of the type became available when the PzKpfw III was up-gunned in 1942.

The complete 8.8cm KwK 43/3 gun from Jagdpanther tank destroyer was also used to establish defensive lines. To mount the weapon required a base to be constructed from wood and concrete; a laborious process which consumed precious materials and manpower. Many were destroyed almost as soon as they been completed, falling victim to enemy artillery or ground-attack aircraft.

The *Westwall* (or Siegfried Line) was established in the years before World War II. After the capitulation of France, the fortification became dormant, but was re-activated in 1944 as Allied forces advanced on Germany. Although considered to be obsolete as an anti-tank gun, the 3.7cm PaK could still provide high-explosive supporting fire.

to reactivate the *Westwall* fortifications; did those responsible realize that they offered little defence against the latest Allied artillery weapons.

As German forces began the long withdrawal from the Eastern Front in 1943, military planners decided to assemble a new type of defensive lines called *Panther-Stellung*; sometimes *Ostwall* (East wall). These would be sited some distance to the rear of the frontline, and positioned so as to take advantage of natural obstacles (lakes and rivers) and previously abandoned fortifications. However, the rapid advances being achieved by the Red Army in the sectors occupied by *Heeresgruppe Mitte* and *Heeresgruppe Süd* did not allow time for such a defensive line to be positioned. In June 1944, *Heeresgruppe Mitte* collapsed as their defensive lines were penetrated in many places.

As the advancing Red Army drew closer to the borders of Poland, Hitler ordered, in March 1944, the establishment of *Feste Plätze*, or *Festungen* (fortresses). Any Polish city considered to be of strategic importance was to be fortified; German military planners saw this as a way to tie-down large numbers of Soviet troops, and hoped it would slow or even halt their advance.

Despite vehement opposition from many German high-ranking officers, an initial 29 cities, along a line from Reval in Estonia to Nikolayev in the Crimea, were to be reinforced as fortresses and involve a considerable

An 8.8cm KwK 43/3 installed in an unfinished – the scaffolding is visible – concrete bunker, part of the desperate attempt to reinforce the defences on the western borders of Germany.

The 10.5cm FlaK 39 was the mainstay of German heavy anti-aircraft artillery. First used to defend German cities and industry facilities against raids by Allied bombers, many were deployed around Berlin as anti-tank guns in an attempt to halt the advancing Soviet tanks.

The barrel, breech and cradle of a 7.5cm PaK 40 have been mounted on a simple concrete base to reinforce part of a static defensive line.

number of German units, a vast amount of ammunition and many tons of construction materials. As an example, the fortress at Vitebsk was manned by three divisions.

Many of the personnel sent to man the fortresses came from penal battalions rather than being experienced or elite troops from crack units and were equipped with obsolete, or in many instances, captured artillery weapons.

Although the concept did not prove effective for slowing the Soviet advance, many more cities, in the east and west, were declared as fortresses by the end of 1944.

Each fortress was to have a *Festungs-PaK-Verbände* (fortress-based anti-tank unit), some 26 of which had been established by end of the war. Each unit was approximately the size of a regiment, and included a staff company and up to ten *Festungs-PaK-Kompanien* (FestPaKKp – fortress-based anti-tank companies).

On 23 December 1944, an order was issued for a further 20 FestPaKKp to be established as detailed in KStN 1147, dated January 1945. This structure was formulated in a very general manner. Each company had a staff section and two platoons, one issued with four m PaK (towed) and another with four s PaK (towed). But an addendum to KStN 1147 shows a wide variation of types available:

Medium PaK: 7.62cm *Infanterie-Kanonen-Haubitze* (InfKanHaub – infantry cannon-howitzer) 290(r), 7.5cm PaK 97/38, *Sockellafette* (Skl – pedestal-type mounting) 1 with 7.5cm K 51, Skl 1 with 7.5cm KwK 67, Skl 1 with 5cm KwK 39, and also the 7.5cm RfK and the 8.8cm RakWrf 43.

Towards the end of the war a number of *Flugzeugabwehrkanone* (FlaK – anti-aircraft gun) units were transferred to the Eastern Front in an attempt to stop the advancing Red Army. Here an 8.8cm FlaK, on an auxiliary gun mount, has been dug-in to serve as an anti-tank artillery piece.

Above: A number of *Pantherturm-Stellung* (panther turret positions) were placed along the *Gotenstellung* (Gothic Line) which had been built across Northern Italy to deny Allied forces access to the cities of Bologna, Milan and Turin.

Right: The top armour of this Panther turret has been reinforced to protect the turret against heavy artillery fire and ground-attack aircraft.

Above: Many of the PzKpfw V Panther turrets deployed had been removed from tanks returned to Germany for repair or major overhaul. While most would be returned to battle, many were also converted as *Bergepanther*, recovery vehicles. The surplus turrets were used to reinforce defensive lines.

Left: A number of *Pantherturm-Stellung* on a railway wagon ready to be transported to reinforce front-line defences. The turret and mounting ring, (possibly from an Ausf D), has been fitted onto a box-like structure fabricated from mild steel. A *Festungskompanie*, (fortress company) was equipped with 12 mountings.

Above: A US soldier examines a 5cm KwK L/42 on a *Behelfs-Sockellafette* (temporary pedestal-type mounting) in a concrete emplacement, part of the Atlantic Wall at Barneville-Carteret, Normandy. The gun would have been effective against landing craft or lightly armoured amphibious vehicles.

Right: A *Panther-Turmstellung* (panther turret position) has been destroyed by the gun crew as they abandoned the site. (NARA)

Heavy PaK: 7.5cm PaK 40 (on wheeled carriage or pedestal mount), 7.62cm PaK 36, 7.62cm PaK 39 and the 8.8cm PaK 43, 43/1, 43/41, or *Pantherturm*.

A light car was authorized, but instead of further motor vehicles only four light and six heavy horses were made available.

The above mentioned 20 FestPaKKp companies were actually equipped with 160 *Puppchen* and 80 8.8cm PaK 43.

Use of Tank Turrets

A good example of how obsolete material could be used is when the 5cm KwK L/42 became obsolete and was replaced in the PzKpfw III by a more powerful 5cm KwK L/60, and a total of 1,800 guns became available. Many of these guns were fitted on a modified *Sockel*-type mounting with a simple armoured gun shield attached. An unknown number of these weapons were installed in the *Atlantikwall*.

An 8.8cm FlaK battery on the Eastern Front in January 1945. FlaK Regiment 47 assembled their weapons as a defensive 'FlaK-*Riegel*' (anti-aircraft gun bar) near Görlitz, on the Polish border. The gun trailers and towing vehicles were parked close by to allow the unit to make a quick retreat.

An 8.8cm FlaK guarding a main road somewhere in the eastern part of the Reich in late 1944. While the gun was a formidable weapon against all enemy tanks, it could fall victim to the latest Soviet tank guns.

Covered by snow, the freezing crew of this early production 8.8cm FlaK (note the target pointer mechanism) prepare their gun for anti-tank combat. Any attempt to defend the gun against attacking enemy infantry would be hopeless, leading to the loss of the gun.

The 10.5cm FlaK 39 heavy anti-aircraft gun was also a formidable low-trajectory support and anti-tank weapon able to defeat all types of Allied tanks.

The use of a tank turret was initiated in 1943, when an inventory of all available stocks had been initiated. A document dated May 1944, notes that over 2,800 turrets of 20 different types were available. Among them were some unusual items: 88 turrets for the *Flammpanzer* (flame-thrower tank) known as the 'Flamingo', 27 from the VK 901 and six VK 3001 turrets. A number of these weapons would be installed in the *Atlantikwall*, some in the *Ostwall* and others in fortified positions to defend important factories.

A production surplus allowed 200 PzKpfw V Panther turrets to be made available for use in defensive emplacements that were fabricated, in the field, from steel, concrete or even wood. The emplacement would be buried in the earth with only the turret visible.

To stop the Allied advance in Italy, it was decided to establish a defensive line north of Rome in late 1943. The *Goten-Stellung* (Gothic Line) was built by making good use of the prevailing terrain. A system of bunkers and dug-in *Pantherturm* (Panther turrets) were positioned over the length of the line, which held until April 1945.

It is interesting to note that 450 of the 8.8cm PaK 43/3 usually installed in the *Jagdpanther* tank hunter were mounted on stationary *Sockel* (pedestal) mounts. According to documents available, all were used on the Western Front.

A unique document dated February 1945, indicates that it was planned to install 50 Henschel-type turrets mounting the 8.8cm KwK 43 (Tiger II) in the *Margarethen-Stellung* (position Margaret) near Lake Balaton in Hungary.

Although having considerable firepower, these immobile guns were, once spotted, vulnerable to well-directed artillery fire or ground-attack aircraft.

On 27 February 1945, General Krebs sent a message to *Heeresgruppe Weichsel*:

> *Festungs-PaK-Verband* XXVI, with ten companies, was assigned to the fortresses at Frankfurt/Oder and Küstrin. It is under the command of IX.*Armee*, but only 1.Kp to 4.Kp are to be stationed in the vicinity of Frankfurt/Oder. The other companies will be deployed in rear areas. According to enquires made in Küstrin only 18 7.5cm PaK 40 and five *Panthertürme* are available and this is considered to be insufficient. We request that this matter is rectified.

It is clear that these 'fortresses' and other defensive lines were the last bastion against the vast formations of the advancing Red Army. The guns on pedestal mounts in fixed positions could be neutralized by well-aimed artillery fire or an attack by experienced infantry. Wheeled anti-tank guns had to be moved by horses.

Survey of Festungs-PaK as of 4 December 1944

Weapons	East			West			Italy
High-grade weapons	Actual	Planned	Sum	Actual	Planned	Sum	Actual
8.8cm PAK 43	208	120	328	85	-	85	?
8.8cm KwK 43/3 *Jagdpanther*	-	-	-	250	200	450	?
8.8cm FLaK (r)	-	-	-	100	-	100	?
7.5cm Pak 40 mot Z	119	-	119	36	-	36	?
7.5cm Pak 40 rotational bedding	-	-	-	300	210	510	?
7.5cm PaK 40 on *Sockel*	-	-	-	-	80	80	?
Pantherturm 7.5cm KwK 42 L/70	-	36	36	63	33	96	48
7.62cm PAK 36	12	-	12	-	-	-	?
7.62cm PaK 39	132	80	212	64	-	64	?
Substandard weapons							
7.62cm IKH 290 (r)	865	72	937	176	-	176	?
7.5cm PaK 97/38	30	-	30	-	-	-	?
7.5cm KwK 67 (5 cm rebored) on *Sockel*	-	400	400	-	300	300	?
5cm KwK 39/1 on *Sockel*	-	180	180	-	150	150	?
8.8cm RW 43 *Puppchen*	168	88	258	-	-	-	?

The end of World War II in Europe: An 8.8cm FlaK on *Behelfslafette* (temporary mounting) has been abandoned and left pointing at the sky; only the Reichstag remains standing in the debris of what had been the city of Berlin.

An 8.8cm FlaK mounted on an *Aushilfslafette* (auxiliary carriage) positioned in a German city to fight enemy armour. The gun is painted *dunkel grau* (dark grey) which indicates that it was in service with a FlaK unit stationed nearby. Note, a shell remains in the fuse setting device, and the large amount of ammunition stacked behind the gun.

High Tech and Austerity 8

By 1943, the *Panzerjäger* had been equipped with very effective anti-tank guns; the result of design and development work that had been initiated in 1941. The 7.5cm PaK 40 was the pre-eminent weapon and the type was issued to establish tank destroyer battalions in infantry and Panzer divisions. Rheinmetall-Borsig designed and manufactured the weapon and had delivered more than 20,000 by the end of the war in Europe.

German anti-tank forces regained superiority when significant numbers of the 8.8cm PaK 43, designed and manufactured by Krupp (also Rheinmetall-Borsig), began to be delivered units on the battlefront. The majority were completed as a conventional towed type, but the weapon was also mounted as a self-propelled tank destroyer that combined excellent mobility with formidable firepower. The 8.8cm PaK 43 is considered by many to have been the best anti-tank gun to enter service in World War II. Some 3,100 guns had been completed by May 1945.

In 1944, the infantry began to receive the *Panzerschreck* and *Panzerfaust*; both were man-portable and effective close-combat weapons which allowed them to defeat enemy tanks. Both types were to replace the anti-tank rifle.

On 6 June 1944, German troops positioned on or near the coast of Normandy came under a massive naval bombardment and heavy bombing by Allied air forces preparatory to an amphibious landing by infantry and supporting armour. The ensuing battles to form a bridgehead and then make the advance into France were characterized by powerful armoured thrusts, carried out at speed by Allied tank forces. Consequently, many German units were forced on the retreat – many fought hard and delayed the advance – and

Adolf Hitler showed great interest in the development of weapons for his military, often attending field demonstrations, of new and projected types, organized by Albert Speer. Here the Führer is receiving a briefing on the ammunition for the new 8.8cm PaK 43 anti-tank gun.

were never allowed time to regroup. Another factor was that the German units occupying were poorly equipped and many units were commanded by officers with little, or no, combat experience leading untrained troops. A truly decisive factor was that Allied combat aircraft had the freedom of the skies over the battlefront.

On another front, German forces fighting a defensive (strategic) retreat in the east were under constant attack from a Red Army, fielding what seemed to them a never-ending number of tanks followed by massed infantry and supported by heavy artillery. On 23 June 1944, Soviet forces launched their *Belorusskya Nastupatelnya Operatsiya* (Belorussian Strategic Offensive Operation), code name Bagration, which was to lead to *Heeresgruppe Mitte* being cut-off from *Heeresgruppe Nord Ukraine* and almost annihilated

After D-Day:

In July 1944, the GenInspdPzTrp commented on the experiences of anti-tank forces fighting in Normandy and compiled by *Oberst* Oemichen:

Main issues:

1.)
All the available experiences in regard to fighting Allied tanks refer to the period from 6 to 24 June 1944. The majority of the fighting took place in the hedgerow [bocage] and bush-covered terrain which typifies Normandy. The commitment seen here is a bush war, which affects how the enemy deploys his tanks, and how they are defended. However, due to the terrain being unique to the region, any experience gained here cannot be applied to other battlefronts.

3.) Enemy tanks

We can confirm that only a few new types of enemy tanks have been observed:

– The British Cruiser Tank Mk VII Cromwell
– An improved type of the US General Sherman [M4A-4]

The new Cruiser Tank Mk VII Cromwell is a hybrid and uses the turret of a Churchill and the hull and running gear of a Cruiser Tank Mk VI Crusader. The tank is armed with a 5.7cm gun [QF 6-pounder] or alternatively with a 9.5cm *Haubitze* [QF 95mm howitzer]. Its amour is considerably stronger than that of the Crusader, but weaker than that of the Churchill, and can be penetrated by our 5cm anti-tank guns.

The Churchill heavy tank is no longer being used as a main battle tank. But a number of special versions are in service with Allied assault engineers.

The US-built M4 Sherman is to be thought of as the T-34 of the west. The latest version has been improved with better ordnance and armour protection. However, despite having increased armour the Sherman can be destroyed by 7.5cm PaK at medium and long range, and by 5cm PaK at close range.

Deployment of the air-portable light tank Tetrarch has not been confirmed. Despite the many rumours, the 57-ton heavy tank M6 'Dreadnought' has not been encountered. [This refers to the Heavy Tank M6A2-E1 which was rejected by Eisenhower for D-Day, and then cancelled in December 1944]. Conclusion: The anti-tank troops must receive concentrated training on how to defeat the M4 Sherman and the Cromwell Mk VII.

Deployment of enemy tanks after landing:

13.
Contrary to any experiences gained in Sicily, the enemy deployed his tanks as close support to assist his infantry advance. The decision to position the

In 1934, AEG announced that it had developed an *ultrarot* (infrared) image converter to allow vision in complete darkness, and later demonstrated it to WaPrüf 8 in 1936. Development continued and the first *ultrarot* devices were delivered for troop trials in 1942. Here a Marder II, from a training and replacement unit, has been fitted with the brackets to carry the 'headlamp' for the *Ultrarot-Geräte* (UR – infrared equipment). The crew has named the vehicle *Sperber* (sparrow hawk).

majority of our anti-tank capable weapons in concrete emplacements proved to be correct. The weapons were also used to fire on landing craft.

Own anti-tank defences:

25.)

Our *Jagdpanzer* and *Sturmgeschütz* held the advantage when fighting in the sunken lanes and thick hedgerow found in Normandy. Unlike a tank crew, the crews of these self-propelled guns are trained to fight autonomously or as a small unit. In many instances this proved to be advantageous. But both types have limited gun traverse and a low firing height, which restricts deployment in the terrain found in rural Normandy.

Conclusion: It is essential that any action must be pre-planned. More must be deployed to protect the flanks of an attack.

A Marder II fitted with the UR equipment. The item annotated 'b' is the 36cm UR 'headlamp', and item 'a' is the image converter (Braun tube).

26.)

The columns of our PaK mot-Z [motor-towed anti-tank guns] are severely restricted by the hedgerow terrain. If the enemy attacks, only the first or second gun can be brought into action. Furthermore, due to being somewhat difficult

to manoeuvre a unit can be easily targeted by enemy artillery or by marauding ground-attack aircraft.

Conclusion: A column of towed PaK must be widely spaced when travelling and when called to into action kept close to the road or track. Any combat against tanks in the hedgerows, must always be the responsibility of an infantry equipped with man-portable anti-tank weapons.

27.)

The deployment of PaK mot-Z in open terrain is more promising, as demonstrated by the s PzJgAbt in 21.PzDiv in a recent action. The commander ignored regulation combat doctrine and dispersed his towed 8.8cm PaK were over a relatively wide area to take advantage of their long-range performance. Also, the guns were sited able to support and cover each other. The guns were carefully hidden, with the camouflage kept in place even during a change of fire position. These were made at a very slow speed in order not to give the impression of 'rolling bushes' to the distant enemy.

Thanks to this effective camouflage, our losses were small, despite being attacked by heavy enemy artillery fire.

The fighting compartment of the Marder II showing the *Ultrarot-Gerate* installation. The equipment entered production in 1943 and was designated *Zielfernrohr-Geräte* (ZG-sighting equipment) 1221. It is thought that some 1,000 installations had been delivered by Spring 1944.

28.)

It is noted that close-combat anti-tank weapons were used to significant effect; 108 out of a total of 537 enemy tanks destroyed. Although such statistics must be viewed with some reservation, both the *Panzerschreck* and *Faustpatrone* proved to be most effective in the unique terrain found in Normandy.

Conclusion: Development and production of close-combat armour-piercing weapons has to be given the highest priority. Also, range and accuracy must be improved.

The comments in this report regarding the 'new' types of British and US tanks are inaccurate and simply wrong.

All references to German anti-tank defences, made by *Oberst* Oemichen, are simple and very matter of fact, to which the GenInspdPzTrp has added his, somewhat, trivial comments. Apparently *Generalleutnant* Wolfgang Thomale anticipated more landing operations and viewed the invasion of Normandy as one attempt which could be halted. How wrong he was.

However, the report does indicate that German anti-tank defences, when correctly and skilfully deployed, were tactically superior and had more effective weaponry when compared to Allied forces.

German high command was not only strategically unprepared but also tactically; many (particularly heavy) units were positioned a long distance from Normandy, while others were being rested then re-equipped and others just inadequately equipped. Any small success would be simply nullified by superior enemy forces; a situation often faced by German troops fighting on both the Eastern and the Western Fronts.

On the Eastern Front

A lack of information only allows a partial assessment of how well German tank destroyer units performed and how effective they were in combat. The little information available refers to a number of smaller units only, making an overall view impossible.

In January 1944, 101.InfDiv submitted an interesting after-action report:

On 8 January, the division including the newly arrived combat elements (three infantry battalions and two artillery battalions) received orders from PzAOK 1 to march from the Voronozivy area south of Vinnyzja toward Brazlaw. At 07:00hrs, we received a telephone message ordering us to block and defend the fork in the road near Pissarevka to prevent the enemy breaking through towards the west.

In order to guard the two main roads, the three available battalions were positioned in a line east of Voronovizy; the rest were sent to a forest east of Pissarevka. The recently unloaded reconnaissance battalion was immediately ordered to positions near Telepenki to fill the gap between us and the 4.GebDiv.

Although the enemy assault was expected, it still came as a surprise. We had barely reached our planned defensive line, when the leading tank was hit and the advance halted.

After a reconnaissance it became clear that our own weak forces would soon have to fight a superior enemy tank unit which massed along what was to have been our defensive line.

The division had only eight s PaK in PzJgAbt 101 and three s PaK in 16.InfReg 228, which were positioned at two focal points. Our infantry was spread over the rest of the 16km wide frontline and had only close-combat anti-tank weapons.

Each battalion had two to three *Ofenrohre* and also large numbers of *Faustpatrone*. But due to a serious shortage, our close-combat troops did not receive any instruction, nor were they trained on how to aim and fire both of these weapons. Furthermore, the division did not have any self-propelled anti-tank guns or assault guns. A StuG battery was expected overnight from 16.PzDiv.

At around 19:00hrs, the enemy launched his attack with 40 tanks along a narrow strip, which followed the road from Gumenoie. The four anti-tank guns positioned there successfully stopped the assault – the enemy managed to recover four of the tanks. As darkness fell, the enemy turned south and attacked *PaK-Kampfgruppe* (a 5cm PaK and two 3.7cm PaK) at Komaroff and silenced the guns without our fierce fire having any visible effects. The enemy tanks entered Komaroff in compact groups and forced 4.Bttr to retreat.

The enemy then launched simultaneous tank attacks, from the north-east, east and south, on Voronowizy, but these were broken up after several of his tanks had been destroyed. To close the gap in the frontline, to the north of Komaroff, the newly arrived II./PzJgAbt 228 was deployed and prepared for a counterattack. Thanks to the leadership of Major Liebmann this turned out to be successful, with two enemy tanks destroyed and Voronowizy was retaken. But the action happened so quickly that our infantry only managed to establish a narrow defensive line and only had a small number of [close-combat] anti-tank weapons available. The bright moonlight allowed our defences to be observed and the enemy attacked again with tanks forcing our infantry to retreat.

The fighting of the previous day had created much confusion, but dawn revealed the reality that the enemy had gained ground, with some 20 tanks in the northern part of Komaroff. Their repeated attacks had forced our infantry to abandon the positions they held and retreat towards *Gruppe* (group) JägRgt 228 commanded by *Oberst* Siebert. The anti-tank elements consisted of a few close-combat weapons and a PzZerstKp, which had been attached to the division in the early hours of the morning.

On 9 January, the division was attached to PzAOK 4 which was immediately ordered to halt the enemy forces advancing on Shmerinka. The commitment required delaying operation, but for us it was a foregone conclusion that an infantry division, without any mobile or close-combat anti-tank weapons, could not be expected to fight any type of delaying action. Everything, including the terrain, was favourable for the enemy to launch a massed tank attack.

We reported our reservations to the Chief of Staff at PzAOK 4.

During the night of 9 to 10 January, *Gruppe* Siebert escaped from Voronovizy and reached Latanzy without any problems, but they had made random attacks on a number of enemy positions. After fierce fighting in the northern area the *Gruppe* captured the town. Enemy infantry, supported by tanks, made repeated counterattacks. But *Gruppe* Siebert had lost most of its equipment after being continuously under fire from tank guns and artillery. Any possibility of making a break through to the west had virtually disappeared.

Gruppe Siebert had succeeded in tying down a significant number of enemy forces. However, the heavy losses, in men and equipment, suffered by the *Gruppe* was seriously out of proportion to any successes.

When the division realized the true gravity of the situation, it began to prepare a plan for a counterattack. The assault was carried out by a battalion, reinforced with elements of divisional artillery and the heavy weapons from the infantry, and was successful.

The presence of enemy tanks had forced us to attack through the forest, and a fierce and difficult combat developed. Any concentrated attack made by enemy infantry would be annihilated. Our few anti-tank guns kept the enemy tanks at a distance, which allowed *Gruppe* Siebert to retreat.

Conclusion: Commitment of 101.InfDiv in the period 8 to 10 January 1944 has again shown that any combat by an infantry division against large enemy tank formations without adequate anti-tank weapons, will inevitably lead to a significant loss of personnel and valuable equipment.

If the division had been supplied with the authorized strength of 36 anti-tank guns (24 for the PzJgAbt, six each for the PzJgKp in the JägRgt) instead of the 11 actually issued – and if a *Sturmgeschütz* battery had been available from the beginning – the enemy tank assault would have been easily repulsed. Any intrusion into our positions could have been repelled by *Sturmgeschütz* counterattacks.

Without any doubt the close-range weapons – *Faustpatrone* and *Ofenrohr* – are precious weapons for the infantry. It is possible that they will help to establish superiority over the tanks in future. Previously it had not been possible to establish a proper training programme due to the ever-present poor supply of ammunition. If all men are thoroughly trained, they could play a vital role in defensive fighting. However, for offensive operation most close-range anti-tank weapons are not suitable: they could never be a substitute for the *Sturmgeschütz* or a self-propelled anti-tank gun.

The modern-type close-combat anti-tank weapons developed from 1943 onwards for the first time gave the infantry the means to effectively defeat any tank, even the Soviet-built JS-II heavy tank. However, the deployment of a *Panzerschreck* required the gunner to be dangerously close to his target and in range of enemy infantry; it was even more perilous for a *Faustpatrone* gunner who had to operate even closer – quite often his charge would only immobilize his target which would then be attacked by artillery.

After the war, German ingenuity continued to be exploited by many nations, including the Soviet Union, which continued the development of rocket-propelled anti-tank weapons culminating in the highly effective *Ruchnoy Protivotankovy Granatomyot* (RPG – rocket-propelled grenade) 7 series. The Soviets also utilized German technology to produce a medium to long range wire-guided anti-tank missile.

However, the *Waffenamt* continued to issue the specifications for more advanced and sophisticated weapons, but with no regard as to the time it would take to design and develop such items. Again, officials in the *Waffenamt* appear to have disregarded the fact that the German armaments industry was in a parlous state, whereas the German military sought to utilize improved versions of weapons currently in service. Finally a decision was made to modify outdated weaponry as effectively as possible.

7.5cm PaK 37

A large number of 3.7cm PaK were in front-line service in 1943, although it was considered to be obsolete as an anti-tank gun, but front-line troops still appreciated its light weight, which made it easy to manoeuvre in combat. To make best use of these guns the *Waffenamt* made a proposal to replace the 3.7cm gun with a 7.5cm L/21, fitted with a simple muzzle brake, on the same carriage. The weapon fired 7.5cm Gr 38 HL ammunition, the same as the le IG 18, and could penetrate 90mm armour. The high-explosive round was more powerful and had a considerably better effect against a soft target. The 7.5cm gun had a maximum range of 2,700m and 4,500m in indirect fire.

The modification work was so straightforward it could be completed by armourers and engineers in front-line workshops.

The first conversion sets became available in June 1944 and Hitler issued an order for the first 54 to be issued to PzGrenDiv Grossdeutschland (GD) and PzDiv SS-Liebstandarte Adolf Hitler (LAH) for extensive troop trials.

In September 1944, the first sobering after action-reports were published. The *General der Infanterie*, Erich Jaschke, was critical, stating that the gun was inadequate against enemy tanks. The supreme commander Südwest, *Generalfeldmarschall* Albert Kesselring, considered that the gun was unsuitable for infantry tank destroyer companies and should not be issued. In contrast, after-action reports submitted by PzGrenDiv GD noted that the weapon had proven to be effective at between 400m and 1,400m range. It seems that the weapon was very popular with the gunners in PzGrenDiv GD troop.

Interestingly, WaPrüf 4/*Heereswaffenamt* (HWA) issued their reply stating that the modified gun was never intended to be an anti-tank weapon, since it had a low muzzle velocity (345mps), which limited range and seriously affected accuracy. It appears that the HWA had always been completely aware of his fact.

In 1943, military planners found that large numbers of 3.7cm PaK carriages were available and ordered them to be utilized to mount a complete 7.5cm L/21-gun assembly.

The gun was initially designated 7.5cm PaK 37, but in 1944 this was changed to 7.5cm *leichte Infanteriegeschütz* (le IG – light infantry gun) 37. This was more appropriate, underlining the fact its performance had always been similar to that of an infantry support gun. A total of 2,178 were converted by front-line units.

An improved version, the 7.5cm le IG 42, was produced but in far smaller numbers.

7.5cm PaK 50

In a similar approach, the *Waffenamt* discussed improving the performance of the 5cm PaK 38 by boring-out the gun barrel to 7.5cm. The gun barrel was also shortened and fitted with a simple muzzle brake similar to that used for the 7.5cm le IG 37. It was intended to fire 7.5cm PaK 97/38 ammunition, but this was not feasible and 7.5cm KwK L/24 ammunition was selected.

As with 7.5cm PaK 37 all conversion work would be carried out by armourers and engineers in front-line workshops. Although a number of prototypes were built and went through a series of trials, the weapon did not enter production.

New Ammunition

The production of gun barrels and carriages was both time and resource consuming. Faced by shortages at almost all levels, the *Waffenamt* always attempted to find a cost-effective approach while utilizing the latest technology.

The *Hohlladungen* (shaped-charge) is a typical example of German competence at problem solving. By utilizing shaped-charge technology to

In the first months after the war, army weapon specialists searched through German arsenals and armament manufactures for the designs, prototypes and pre-production new weapons. All were to be sent to the USA for detailed examination and appraisal. One type, the 7.5cm PaK 50 anti-tank gun was discovered at an artillery proving ground where a number were undergoing firing trials. All were fitted with a square-shaped muzzle brake with either three or five-baffles.

The *Panzerabwehrwerfer* (PAW) 600 was an 8.14cm rocket-projectile launcher which used *Hock-Niederduck* (high-low pressure) technology. It was designed to fire the same ammunition as the *Granatewerfer* (mortar) 34; the standard infantry mortar in service with German forces. The intention of the designers was to create a relatively lightweight, but powerful anti-tank weapon.

produce anti-tank ammunition, even outdated weapons, such as the 7.5cm KwK L/24, could be used against the modern Soviet tanks with some chance of success. All other German KwK 40 and StuK 40 were issued with shaped-charge rounds as a supplement to the standard PzGr 39 or, most probably, to conserve precious PzGr 40 ammunition.

Between 1943 and 1944, the *Panzerjäger* had been supplied with high-performance weapons which had sufficient firepower to destroy most types of enemy tank at all ranges, but mobility in the vicinity of the frontline remained a problem.

The divisional anti-tank battalion was normally used as a mobile force to engage the enemy at all ranges, and was often deployed to establish a focal point in the defensive line. Under normal circumstances these units could change firing position with only an occasional hold up. But the question of mobility was eased when units were equipped with self-propelled guns, and sometime later the *Sturmgeschütz*.

The gun crews in regimental anti-tank units had to reposition their gun by using only muscle power; it was critical for the weight of any new weapon to be kept to a minimum. When the 7.5cm PaK 40 entered service, anti-tank units now had a weapon able to defeat, but the weapon weighed some 1,425kg.

The development and introduction into service of the *Panzerschreck* and *Panzerfaust* was an important step since it provided front-line troops with lightweight man-portable anti-tank weapons.

However, these weapons were only effective at 100m to 150m range. It is understandable that the *Waffenamt* was desperate to fill the gap between the light weapons and the heavy anti-tank guns.

Fortunately, Krupp had been developing hoch und niederdruck (high and low pressure) technology and were in the process of applying this to the development of a high-powered anti-tank weapon.

PAW 600

This weapon had an 8.14cm fin-stabilized projectile, with a ring charge of powerful propellant wrapped around the fins, which was loaded into a massive breech block. When ignited the weapon did not fire immediately, but once maximum pressure had built up in the breech the projectile was launched. Although it had a relatively low muzzle velocity (520mps), it had a maximum range of 6,200m when firing high-explosive ammunition

PAW 600 and contemporary German anti-tank weapons					
	8.8cm RW 43 *Puppchen*	7.5cm le IG 37	7.5cm PaK 40	8.8cm PaK 43	PAW 600
Calibre	8.8cm	7.5cm	7.5cm	8.8cm	8.14cm
Barrel length	1,600mm	?	3,450mm = L/46	6,585mm = L/71	2.4m/3m (Krupp/Rheinmetall)
Effective range (maximum)	700m	5,150m (HE)		14,200m (HE)	6,000m firing HE
Muzzle velocity	110mps	355mps (HI round)	990mps (PzGr 40)	1,140mps (PzGr 40)	520mps
Firing height	?	745mm		1,100mm	800mm
Side traverse	?	60°	65°	360°	80°
Elevation range	-8° to +40°	-5 to +24°	- 5° to + 22°	-8° to +40°	32°
Rate of fire	10rpm	?	10–15rpm	10rpm	?
Weight in travelling mode	149kg	510kg	1,425kg	5,400kg	600kg
Weight in firing position	105kg	510kg	1,425kg	3,700kg	600kg
Armour penetration 100m	160mm up	75–90mm up	100mm (PzGr 40)	250mm* (PzGr 40)	140mm up
Armour penetration 1,000m	to 700m	to 1,000m	87mm	193mm*	to 800m
Armour penetration 1,500m	–	–	82mm	170mm*	–
Armour penetration 4,000m	–	–	–	80mm	–

* Document gives diverging data to other files

Both Rheinmetall and Krupp were contracted to design and produce prototypes for a 12.8cm dual-purpose (field/anti-tank) gun. The Rheinmetall version was mounted on an elaborate carriage – which allowed all-round traverse – with three axles carried on torsion-bar suspension.

and an effective anti-tank range of 750m when firing shaped-charge ammunition.

The PAW 600 had many advantages over a conventional anti-tank gun. It was simple and cost efficient to manufacture; the gun barrel was not rifled and since the recoil was very weak, a well-constructed carriage would not be required. As a result, the weapon weighed 640kg, but was heavier than a 3.7cm PaK.

Both Krupp and Rheinmetall-Borsig were individually contracted to design and produce a weapon which had to be ready for firing trials in September 1944. The gun was designated *Panzerabwehr-Waffe* (PAW – anti-tank weapon) 600, with suffix letter to identify the manufacturer. The gun utilized a sighting telescope from the s PaK with an integrated *Aushilfs-Richtmittel* (expedient artillery-laying device) 38.

Both weapons were mounted on a simple lightweight *Einheits-Spreizlafette* (standard-type split-trail carriage), which was also to be used on a number of new weapons, including the 7.5cm le IG 42 and a *Nebelwerfer* rocket launcher.

An *Oberstleutnant* Haymann (occupying the post of *General der Infanterie*) emphasized that the PAW was urgently required for front-line service and that it must be given priority over the proposal to increase production of the 7.5cm le IG37. Haymann stated that front-line units required an effective anti-tank weapon, not another infantry gun with limited performance against enemy armour.

Firing trials of the PAW 600 were successful and planning began for the production of the weapon.

A PAW 600 was examined by the Führer at a demonstration of weapons under development. Hitler was delighted to witness 140mm of amour being penetrated with sufficient accuracy, then later being assured by engineers, that an increase to 160mm was feasible.

Following the demonstration, the production of an '0'-series of some 100 PAW was suggested, for military planners to approve. Documents dated February 1945 indicate that a total of 160 PAW 600 were completed.

Both Krupp and Rheinmetall-Borsig went on to develop a 10.5cm version, designed to penetrate 200mm armour, mounted on the carriage of a PaK 38. The result was a weapon that was deemed to be far too heavy for front-line service and did not progress beyond the prototype stage.

The PAW 600 was never intended nor designed to be mounted in a tank.

12.8cm Kanone 81

The development of the 12.8cm K 81 began in 1939, when military planners first issued a requirement for a heavy *Betonknacker* (bunker buster). The type was to be armed with a low-trajectory heavy gun based on the 12.8cm FlaK 40. Design and all development work was completed in 1942, with two guns mounted on the chosen chassis (VK 3001) and prepared for field trials.

Although these vehicles proved to be a failure, the 12.8cm gun was selected for other applications:

- Krupp designed a 12.8cm L/55 gun for the planned Porsche Typ 205 heavy tank (commonly called *Maus*).
- This gun, designated 12.8cm PaK 80, was chosen for the heavy *Sturmgeschütz* (*Jagdtiger*).
- A modern 12.8cm field gun in a cruciform carriage, both Krupp and Rheinmetall-Borsig were contracted to produce trial weapons.

The specification called for a modern low-trajectory field gun, suitable for use as a heavy artillery weapon and also as a heavy anti-tank gun. The gun was to be towed by a SdKfz 7 or SWS when issued to infantry divisions and by an SdKfz 8 for motorized (PzDiv, InfDiv [mot]) units. Firing trials for the 12.8cm cannon were scheduled to commence in July 1944.

Although large-scale production had been planned, both Rheinmetall-Borsig and Krupp proved to be unable to meet the schedule. Since the weapon was regarded to be vitally important, officials at the *Waffenamt* decided, in mid-

Above: The Krupp version was mounted on a more conventional four-wheeled carriage which also allowed all-round fire. The 12.8cm gun on both versions was fitted with a cylindrical multi-perforated muzzle brake.

Right: The Krupp gun differed in that it could be quickly lifted off the carriage by using two hand-operated jacks. The 12.8cm gun had a very impressive performance; firing high-explosive ammunition it had a maximum range of 25km. But the weapon was considered too heavy for use as an anti-tank gun, since its weight would severely limit mobility.

1944, to utilize surplus guns destined for *Jagdtiger* production and mount them on carriages captured from the enemy. For an unknown reason, two different types of split-trail carriage were utilized; that of the French-built 15.5cm K 419(f) and the Soviet-built 15.2cm KH 433(r). The version mounted on a K 419(f) carriage was designated 12.8cm K 81/1 and that on a KH 433(r) the 12.8cm K 81/2.

On 28 October 1944, the OrgAbt ordered the establishment of six 12.8cm batteries, each equipped with six guns, and a deployment guide was published seven days later.

A battery could be issued with either the K 81/1 or the K 81/2 and a number of SdKfz 8 tractors, but due the almost impossible supply situation only two would be issued to each battery. The allotment of five cargo trucks to each battery was totally inadequate, making it almost impossible to replenish ammunition during an artillery exchange. Also, the batteries would have to cooperate with the artillery battalions to receive supplies and mechanical maintenance.

Although the 12.8cm gun had a maximum range of some 24,400m, it could be used against enemy armour; performance data indicates that it could penetrate 150mm armour at a range of 1,000m.

An inventory of all available artillery forces dated February 1945, shows that only three *Heeres-Artillerie-Batterien* (HArtBttr – army artillery batteries) were equipped with 12.8cm K 81/1 (HArtBttr 1092, 1093 and 1097). Whereas three army heavy artillery batteries, HArtBttr 1094, 1095 and 1096 had not been issued with 12.8cm, but instead received 12.2cm guns, possibly captured Soviet 12.2cm K 390-2(r).

In the final months of the war, Krupp and Rheinmetall-Borsig delivered the prototypes of the 12.8cm K 44, but it was too late and neither was accepted for series production.

	12.8cm K 44 (Krupp)	12.8cm K 44 (Rheinmetall)
Calibre	12.8cm	12.8cm
Barrel length		
Effective range (maximum)	24,400m	24,400m
Muzzle velocity	920mps	
Side traverse	360°	360°
Elevation	-5° to +45°	-5° to +45°
Weight with wheels	10,160kg (approx)	10,160kg (approx)
Weight without wheels	?	?
Armour penetration 1,000m	150mm	150mm

Data incomplete, taken from US sources, not verifiable

Conclusion 9

In January 1945, the situation in the Reich continued to deteriorate. Allied and Soviet forces had crossed the borders of the Fatherland, forcing the German military to take desperate measures to stabilize the situation on all fronts.

The PzAOK.3 (3.Panzer Army high command) received this somewhat terse teletype message:

> For combat along the *Kurische Haff/Nehrung* [Curonian Lagoon/Spit] front, 3.Panzer Army will be issued the following weapons:
> 21 – 3.7cm PaK
> Nine – 4.5cm PaK(r)
> 50 – 4.7cm PaK(f)
> 50 – 2cm KwK tank guns
> 100 – 3.7cm KwK tank guns

German forces defending Courland had been cut off from *Heeresgruppe Nord* (Army Group North) since October 1944. After Hitler declared the peninsula 'a fortress', the still effective German forces were to be known as *Heeresgruppe Kurland* (Army Group Courland). All ammunition and other supplies had to be transported from the only available harbour at Libau [Liepāja]. The weapons listed were mainly obsolete types and are indicative of the desperate supply situation.

On 24 January 1945, *Heeresgruppe Weichsel* (Army Group Vistula) was formed as the intended last line of defence between the massed Soviet forces and their objective; the city of Berlin.

July 1944: A Marder III Ausf M tank destroyer has been left immobilized after an Allied bombing attack on German forces positioned in a town near the coast of Normandy. (Getty)

This telex message was sent by *Heeresgruppe Kurland* in January 1945. It details the anti-tank weapons they have available; all, without exception, are outdated or obsolete types captured from French and Russian forces.

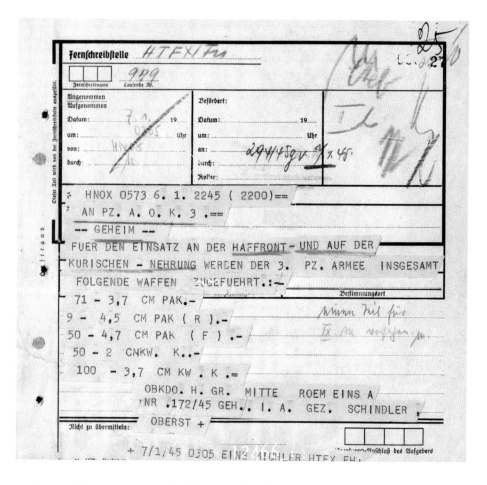

A week later, a group led by a staff officer – name and rank unknown – responsible for anti-tank defence in *Heeresgruppe Weichsel* visited a number of 2.*Armee* units, positioned to hold the line, to evaluate the situation.

We visited the headquarters and front-line troops of the following:
AOK 2 in Preussisch Stargard.
XXIII *Armeekorps* in Schwarzwald.
5.JägDiv in Milwe.
XXVII *Armeekorps* in Rohlau.
XVI PzKorps (SS) in Hammerstein.

1. Active defence

The anti-tank defences are troubled by the constant shortage of fuel and ammunition. There are insufficient anti-tank weapons available. Front-line troops refuse to use weapons such as *Festungs-PaK* or PaK *mot-Zug*. The success

rate of towed PaK is outweighed by the number of losses, the result is that crews have no faith in their weapons. The PzJgAbt at divisional level must be issued with an increased number of either *Sturmgeschütz* or *Selbstfahrlafette* [self-propelled] guns. We suggest issuing two companies with *Sturmgeschütz* and one with 2cm FlaK; sufficient personnel are available. The towed heavy PaK should be transferred to each 14.Kp [in divisional regiments], but towed by SdKfz 11 half-track vehicles rather than the *Rauppenschlepper Ost*.

Recently, 28 *Sturmgeschütz* were unloaded at Konitz and delivered to 4.PzDiv, but they were not fitted with radio equipment and consequently their operational readiness is limited. Any combat operations by 4.PzDiv are further delayed, since workshop elements are hindered by the intermittent supply situation and simultaneous problems with rail transport operated by 'germanische Freiwillige' [North European volunteer units].

The number of tank kills using close-combat weapons has decreased: the reason is that enemy tanks will not approach our defensive lines until artillery or infantry has eliminated our anti-tank teams. Nevertheless, the true value of our close-combat weapons is generally accepted by the troops. The *Panzerfaust* was initially issued in a very arbitrary manner, but it has been decided that it will now be provided to only fully-trained close-combat teams and tactical deployment must be improved. The *Panzer-Zerstörer-Verbände* (PzZerstVerb – tank destroyer group) were partly

In the last months of World War II, the situation for German forces became so desperate that many *Volksgrenadier* and infantry units were equipped with outdated weapons like this 4.5cm PaK 184(r). Vast numbers of these guns had been captured in the first days of *Unternehmen* Barbarossa in June 1941 and were almost useless against Allied and Soviet armour.

deployed as infantry, but with little success and suffering high losses. As an example, *Panzer-Zerstörer-Bataillon* (PzZerstBtl – tank destroyer battalion) 474 had to repulse enemy attacks from 14 to 16 January, but because the unit was not equipped with suitable weapons, they were forced to expend all their *Panzerschreck* ammunition. On 16 January at 14:30hrs, the enemy attacked again with 40 tanks supported by assault guns, but all ammunition had been expended, the anti-tank ditch was crossed and our positions penetrated. Our 2cm FlaK unit fired at the flanks of the enemy attack, but was soon overcome. Due to this essential unit being ineptly deployed it was unable operate as intended and as a result was almost annihilated.

In conclusion, I confirm that the troops demand more *Sturmgeschütz*, but these must be radio equipped and be supplied with sufficient ammunition and fuel. Many of our tanks had to be abandoned and destroyed due to the ever-present shortage of fuel.

2. Passive anti-tank defence

Permission to dig *Panzergraben* [anti-tank ditches] is in general refused; the amount of work required is not commensurate with any benefit. Also, the shortage of weapons does not allow these ditches to be constantly monitored.

A strength report for the period 14 January to 3 February notes that 3.PzArmy had a complement of 23 PzKpfw IV, three PzKpfw V Panther,

During the retreat from the Soviet Union in 1944, 5.SS-PzDiv Wiking captured a number of *Samokhodnaya Ustanovska* (SU – self-propelled installation) 76 from the Red Army. Since the vehicles were in good working order, many were completely repainted and integrated into the PzJgAbt.

two PzKpfw VI Tiger, some 50 *Sturmgeschütz* and 20 *Jagdpanzer* IV. It also had a total of 92 heavy anti-tank guns (mainly 7.5cm PaK 40), ten self-propelled anti-tank guns and also ten 8.8cm PaK.

The report seems to be incomplete, but this is not surprising given the confused and desperate state of German defences in the last days of World War II. But there were successes: PzJgAbt 5 destroyed eight enemy tanks for the loss of eight PaK 40; *Sturmgeschütz* from PzJgKp 1005 destroyed 44 tanks for the loss of two StuG, and StuGBrig 190 destroyed 84 enemy tanks for the loss of 11 StuG.

These figures are not representative of all battlefront actions, but they do show that well-trained *Panzerjäger*, when using the appropriate tactics, could still defeat enemy armour.

At the same time modern close combat units equipped with *Panzerfaust* and *Panzerschreck* were formed. Both had proven their effectiveness on the battlefield, giving the infantry a proven device to destroy any tank on short ranges up to 150m. Especially the small hand-held *Panzerfaust* should revolutionize warfare.

In 1943, the *Panzerjäger* finally began to be issued with effective self-propelled anti-tank guns and were now able to fight the highly mobile tank formations fielded by the Red Army. But, the long-existent problems in the German armaments industry meant that these would never be available in sufficient numbers. Consequently, many *Panzerjäger* units were being forced to continue fighting enemy armour with their towed anti-tank guns.

At the same time as the self-propelled guns were being issued, close-combat units equipped with *Panzerfaust* and *Panzerschreck* were being formed

A Panther-*Turmstellung* buried under the cobble stone surface of a street in a German city. The turret is from a PzKpfw V Ausf D.

The desperate situation faced by German forces at the end of 1944 required them to take desperate measures. Here engineers have constructed a 'self-propelled gun' by mounting a 7.5cm StuK 40, removed from a damaged *Sturmgeschütz*, on the chassis of an obsolete PzKpfw I Ausf B.

in the infantry. Both weapons proved to be very effective on the battlefield, allowing German infantry to destroy or immobilize an enemy tank at up to 150m range. The compact hand-held *Panzerfaust* revolutionized anti-tank warfare in World War II.

Towards end of the war, German engineers were working on the development of a wire-guided anti-tank missile. The Ruhrstahl X-7 had an effective range of some 1,200m, and was designed fill the gap between a short-range (handheld or man-portable) anti-tank weapon and a conventional anti-tank gun.

In 1943, the *General der Panzertruppe* decided to branch off a large number of assault guns [*Sturmgeschütz*], and made a decision to supply them to the Panzer divisions and PzGrenDiv waiting to receive replacement tanks. A significant number were also issued the *Panzerjäger* to equip their anti-tank battalions in infantry and tank divisions.

The *Sturmgeschütz* had always been a vital support weapon for the infantry and when the StuG IV armed with a 7.5cm KwK 40 L/48 – later a 7.5cm KwK 42 L/70 in the Pz IV/70(A) and Pz IV/70(V) – entered service they soon had a most effective tank destroyer. The history of German assault guns is detailed in: *Sturmartillerie, Osprey Publishing: 2016 and Sturmgeschütz, Osprey Publishing: 2017.*

By the end of World War II, the German anti-tank force had had come to the end of a long journey since being formed in 1918. It was originally established by the *Reichswehr* as the *Panzerabwehrtruppe* and operated as a dedicated defensive force; a role that was maintained until the formation of the *Wehrmacht* on 16 June 1935. However in 1939, the name of the force was changed to *Panzerjäger*, indicating that it was now to be deployed in an offensive role. At the same, their weapons were re-designated; the *Panzerabwehrkanone* became the *Panzerjägerkanone*. Their intended role as tank hunters worked well until 1941, but their anti-tank weapons were approaching obsolescence. New weapons had to be designed and developed to defeat more modern – better armed and armoured – tanks entering the battle on the *Ostfront*. But, well trained and combat-experienced *Panzerjäger* continued to be feared by many Red Army tank crews. When German anti-tank forces received the s PaK in 1942, a relative parity was reached, but this would be short-lived, since the enemy continued with the development of heavier, highly mobile and better-armed tanks.

As the campaign in the east progressed, the Red Army began to deploy these improved types in massed formations and use their mobility to full advantage; unfortunately German towed anti-tank guns were not equally mobile. The commanders of all *Panzerjäger* units involved in the fighting were aware of what type of weapon was required; a highly-mobile self-propelled anti-tank gun. But military planners were yet to issue a specification for such a weapon and subsequently issued no development contracts.

A simple solution would have been to adapt the turretless, armoured assault gun, which had been in service since 1940, by mounting the type with an effective high-performance gun. This eventually happened in 1943/44, and the vehicles were successfully deployed as *Panzerjäger* which in turn led to the development of even more powerfully armed self-propelled, turretless, heavily-armoured tank hunter-killer vehicles: *Jagdpanzer* IV; *Jagdpanzer* 38(t); *Jagdpanther* and eventually the super-heavy *Jagdtiger*.

The *Panzerjäger* in the frontline, however, would be forced to continue to fight using towed or portable anti-tank weapons until end of the war. The *Panzerabwehrkanone* and *Panzerfaust* were the synonymous to the *Landser* (everyday name for a German soldier) as the only hope against the onslaught of ever-growing masses of Russian tanks.

Afterword

It is almost impossible to fully assess the effectiveness and performance of German *Panzerjäger* (tank hunter) units due to a lack of relevant records. Any information available refers to only small units, and does not give an overview.

The crew of this 5cm PaK 38 has effectively concealed their gun in the snow-covered landscape; even wheels are covered with white blankets. The gun is in service with 14. *Waffen-Grenadier-Division*, an SS unit manned by Galician (West Ukranian) volunteers. (Getty)

Opinion varies as to the point in time when Germany actually lost the war: was it the failure of *Unternehmen* Barbarossa leading to defeat at the gates of Moscow; the catastrophe at Stalingrad; the failed Kursk salient offensive and the virtual annihilation of *Heeresgruppe Mitte*? Or was the truly decisive moment when Allied forces landed on the beaches of Normandy on 6 June 1944?

The situation faced by German troops became increasingly parlous in the last months of the war. A lack of large operational units forced commanders, with almost fanatical zeal, to establish defined lines of defence or *feste Plätze* (fortress sites). The long battle for the Kurland (Courland) peninsula in Latvia is indicative of such a senseless struggle.

On 16 October 1944, the Red Army overran Riga and a few days later their units pushed north to capture the important ports of Libau (Liepaja) and Windau (Ventspils). German defenders in the area were still effective and determined to break through to East Prussia. But following orders from Hitler, *Generaloberst* Schörner, the fanatical commander of the newly formed *Heeresgruppe Kurland* (Army Group Courland) prevented any attempt to break out: *Festung* (Fortress) *Kurland* had to be held at all costs.

A number of documents produced by s H PzJgAbt 667 illustrates the situation. The unit had been established on 19 July 1943 as one of 18 independent heavy tank-destroyer units. The battalion was equipped with 36 8.8cm PaK 43/41, which had once equipped other units trapped on the peninsula.

Vienna, April 1944: in the background are the 7.5cm PaK 40 anti-tank guns, towed by SdKfz 250, of a PzJg unit. The officer is General von Bünau, who was *Kampfkommandant* (military commander) of the Austrian capital until the end of the war.

Ready for destruction: A stack of various types of man-portable German anti-tank weapons collected by US troops, includes *Panzerfaust* 60m and the improved *Panzerfaust* 100m.

In October 1944, the second battle for the control of Kurland was fought, during which the Red Army lost more than 1,000 armoured vehicles. A brief and somewhat deceptive period of calm followed, during which the commander of German II.*Armeekorps* ordered all units to intensify training for anti-tank defence.

The commanding officer of s H PzJgAbt 667 implemented these orders, and all personnel, from gunners to drivers of supply trucks, received intensive training in how to fight with infantry weapons, and in the use of close combat anti-tank weapons.

The unit could not leave its positions and assembly areas until mid-December 1944, since the completely sodden ground made many areas impassable. On 16 December, all three combat companies of the battalion were attached to II.*Armeekorps*.

Both 1.Kp and 2.Kp were sent to support 132.InfDiv and 225.InfDiv and moved into positions to the rear of the frontline near Videlotis; 3.Kp was held in reserve ready to move up and attack any enemy tanks which had managed to break through the line.

The third battle of Kurland began on 20 December 1944, just as a severe frost settled over the battlefront. The first attack was made by Red Army infantry supported by a force of JS-2 heavy tanks; four were defeated by the guns of s H PzJgAbt 667 at between 1,000m and 1,500m range.

In December, 2.Kp noted that it had lost six 8.8cm Pak 43/41 and one 7.92mm *Maschinengewehr* (MG – machine gun) 42 in an after-action report:

Despite mobility problems, heavy field artillery units were often called on to defeat an attack by enemy armour. The s 10cm K18 could defeat any enemy tank – but would always be at risk of being targeted by enemy artillery.

On 21 December 1944, at 08:00hrs, the enemy attacked with infantry supported by tanks and fighter aircraft, in the area near Pampali and Saldus, and succeeded in pushing our front-line troops to beyond the gun emplacements. The preliminary heavy barrage (artillery and bombs) left five guns so badly damaged that they could no longer be used. But one gun was able to shoot and managed to defeat two enemy tanks, before being attacked and heavily damaged by an enemy flamethrower tank.

Later that afternoon, and again in the early hours on the morning of 22 December, we made an attempt to recover the guns at the same time as our troops launched a counterattack. But we failed since the Russians had not been flushed from their positions.

On 10 January 1945, an unknown officer noted:

Past combat has shown that neither the platoon leaders, gunners nor individual soldiers had any knowledge of what was detailed in the combat orders. I therefore suggest that battle orders are distributed before any combat.

Six days later the battalion received surprising instructions:

To s H PzJgAbt 667:
The battalion is ordered to Mielau (Mława) for conversion training with assault;

all current personnel and their equipment are involved, but the s PaK and any half-track tractors are to remain. The battalion is to be transferred by rail transport to the area east of the port of Libau and prepare to embark on a ship. The notification has been sent immediately to the *Oberquartiermeister* at Libau. The 13 s PaK and half-track tractors remaining from s H PzJgAbt 667 are to be delivered to PzJgAbt 752. The guns are to be left in their present positions.

However, the battalion did not ship-out but was ordered to establish *Panzerjagdkommandos* (tank destroyer squads) armed with RakPzB 54/1 (*Panzerschreck*) – as ordered by army high command – to defend various locations if they were attacked by Red Army forces. Apparently, the intention to transport the battalion by sea to the west was delayed several times and it remains unknown as to whether the unit was actually transferred to Mielau.

This tabular material was attached to the above after-action report:

10 *Tage-Meldung* (ten day report) s PzJgAbt 667

Date	8.8cm PaK 43/41	8.8cm PaK 43	MG 42/MG 34
1 December 1944	16	7	30
11 December 1944	16	7	30
21 December 1944	17	7	30
1 January 1945	4	3	24
11 January 1945	5	4	24
21 January 1945	5	5	24

The unit was re-armed with *Panzerschreck*:

10 *Tage-Meldung* (ten day report) s PzJgAbt 667

Date	RakPzb 54/1	MG 42
31 January 1945	85	4
11 February 1945	83	4
21 February 1945	83	4

Despite being armed with highly effective 8.8cm PaK 43 anti-tank guns, s PzJgAbt 667 operated dangerously close to the frontline. In an emergency situation it was often impossible to make safe retreat, subsequently the unit suffered substantial losses.

It is very likely that after being ordered to operate as tank destroyer squads, the loss of personnel considerably increased.

By the end of the war in 1945, a further three battles for the Kurland peninsula had been fought.

An abandoned French-built 4.7cm PaK 181(f) in the sand dunes overlooking Omaha Beach. When first captured in 1940, German anti-tank units considered it to be an excellent weapon, but it soon became obsolete. (Getty)

INDEX

Acknowledgements

As with my previous books, I have searched and gathered much original information from a number of public archives, the Bundesarchiv/Militärarchiv in Freiburg, Germany, and the National Archives & Records Administration, Washington, USA. Furthermore the internet-based Project for the Digitizing of German Documents in Archives of the Russian Federation has been used to a great extent.

Only a few post-war publications have been referred to in writing this book. However, *Panzertracts* produced by Tom Jentz and Hilary L. Doyle, is much valued for accuracy.

My sincere thanks to the following individuals who have provided help, advice and also access to their collections:
Florian von Aufseß, Peter Müller (Historyfacts), Karlheinz Münch, Henry Hoppe and Holger Erdmann

Many thanks to John Nelson, who helped by supplying much precious and surprising information.

Finally, sincere thanks to Jasper Spencer-Smith, my ever-patient editor, who conceived the book and worked on my manuscript. Also thanks to Nigel Pell for his excellent layout and Shaun Barrington for preparing the index.

All the images in this book are, unless otherwise identified, from Thomas Anderson's private collection.

Bibliography

Panzertruppen Volume 1 and Volume 2, Tom Jentz, Podzun-Pallas Verlag
Panzertracts, several volumes, Panzertracts, Maryland, USA
Verbände und Truppen der Deutschen Wehrmacht, (16 Volumes), G. Tessin